PRESENTS

CLIMATE CRISIS
CHRONICLES

ETHAN SACKS
Writer

DALIBOR TALAJIĆ
Artist & Cover Artist

LEE LOUGHRIDGE
Colorist & Cover Colorist

BOSUNG KIM
Letterer (Chapters 1–3)

DULCE MONTOYA
Editor & Letterer (Chapters 4–10)

YEONJUNG KIM
Print Conversion

These are true stories.

   @AWA_studios   @awastudiosofficial   @awastudiosofficial 🌐 awastudios.net

Axel Alonso Chief Creative Officer
Matthew Anderson Co-Chair & President
Ariane Baya Financial Controller
Chris Burns Production Editor
Ramsee Chand AWA Studios Assistant
Thea Cheuk Assistant Editor
Michael Coast Senior Editor
Bob Cohen EVP, General Counsel
Michael Cotton Executive Editor

Chris Ferguson Art Director
Frank Fochetta Senior Consultant, Sales & Distribution
Anne Globe Marketing Consultant
Jackie Liu Digital Marketing Manager
Dulce Montoya Associate Editor
Kevin Park Associate General Counsel
Andrew Serwin Managing Editor
Daphney Stephen Accounting Assistant
Zach Studin President, AWA Studios

The forecast calls for a new kind of journalism

This groundbreaking graphic novel represents two passions of mine coming together in ways I could never have imagined. On a basic level, the graphic novel and its progenitor, the comic book, have been a part of my life since I picked up my first *Detective Comics* featuring The Batman when I was eight years old.

At the same time, climate change and its devastating effects on our planet have been at the forefront of my mind for the last three decades. This is personal for me. I have seen first-hand how our planet is reacting to warming oceans and atmosphere.

The biggest challenge for many of us in journalism is how to find ways to bring this story to as many people as possible. How do we reach and engage with global audi-

by
AL ROKER

ences where they live, and how they learn? To meld facts and science with accessible art and storytelling is the next frontier and, frankly, one of those head-smacking "Why didn't I think of that?" moments. But I'm glad somebody has.

This effort is as good as any graphic novel out there right now. And the information it imparts is real, world-class science that also grabs you in a visceral way. I certainly haven't seen this type of storytelling attempted before on this topic.

We hope you are informed, and enlightened. We hope after absorbing this project, you look at our climate in a different way. To borrow a line from one of the Golden Age creators of the graphic arts, Stan Lee, "Excelsior!" Ever upward.

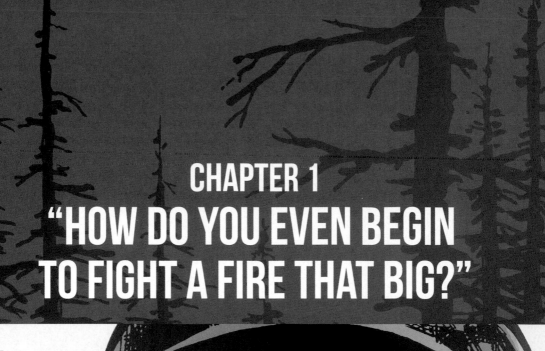

CHAPTER 1
"HOW DO YOU EVEN BEGIN TO FIGHT A FIRE THAT BIG?"

Mark Brunton, 52,
Battalion Chief, Cal Fire

I've been a firefighter for 36 years. I've been on the Cal Fire Incident Management Team for about 20 of them.

Wildfires have been part of the job since I started.

But it really took off in the last five years.

That's when we started seeing fires that were **significantly** bigger.

The Dixie Fire, August, 2021.

We've been in a historic drought for the past few years in California.

We're finding that the vegetation is **very** dry. Conditions that are fuel for bigger wildfires.

I have two different deputy operation supervisors who oversee a huge sector of the fire, and underneath them are branches and the divisions.

We usually start with meetings early in the morning. You get a download from whoever is doing night operations, about what happened overnight.

There's a formal operations briefing for all the resources fighting fire that day. Then it's time to go out and start doing the job for the day.

After the meetings, there's a small window of time for a recon flight.

It gives me a chance to see the sheer power of the fire, how quickly and thoroughly it consumes trees, brush and structures on such a large scale. A recon flight can take well over an hour to fly only a portion of the fire.

I can feel the heat radiate even though I am hundreds of feet above the flames.

By the time my team arrived at the Dixie Fire, it had been burning for weeks.

A lot of the fire was on steep terrain, heavy timber, with unprecedented runs of thousands or tens of thousands of acres burned in a 24-hour period.

None of us had ever seen a fire burn with that intensity.

The backburn fire consumes the fuel between the fireline and the wildfire.

That way, when the wildfire burns up to that area, it runs out of fuel and goes out or it lowers in intensity.

Then we can get in there and use hose-lines to extinguish the flames.

It takes a lot of time, especially if you're in timber. It takes days. Your line has to be quite large. You need a lot of resources to make it work.

The Dixie Fire was the second largest fire in California history, acreage wise, pushing almost a million acres.

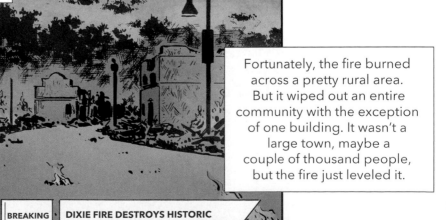

Fortunately, the fire burned across a pretty rural area. But it wiped out an entire community with the exception of one building. It wasn't a large town, maybe a couple of thousand people, but the fire just leveled it.

BREAKING NEWS

DIXIE FIRE DESTROYS HISTORIC CALIFORNIA TOWN OF GREENVILLE

I know the devastation of wildfires all too well.

Last year, in Napa, the fire actually burned down my uncle's home.

That was surreal. When you kind of have a connection to it.

It's a terrible thing to see when there are communities wiped out, but when it becomes a personal thing, that brings it home.

Oh man, I've been in that house. It's pretty devastating.

My son is in the Navy, and while he protects our country, I am protecting our home state from wildfires.

My priority is to keep California safe and to safely return to my family.

That isn't guaranteed. I've had a few close encounters.

In the 2017 Thomas Fire in Southern California, I got cut off by the fire when it just took off. I had to try to make it to one of the preset safety islands.

The fire was burning across the road, but I couldn't see. I had to gun it.

I couldn't remember what the road was like. I just hoped it didn't take a turn, or I'd fly off a cliff.

But I got through it, got to the safety island and basically waited it out for two hours while the fire burned around me. That was close.

Fires now are so much more devasting than they used to be.

It's a grind. The fire season is longer as it gets hotter and drier. You're going from fire to fire. I'll have a day off then it's off to the next one.

It's like Groundhog Day.

You have to take the wins where you get them.

CHAPTER 2
WHEN BACK-TO-BACK HURRICANES DEVASTATE A HONDURAN COMMUNITY

Lucita Hernandez, 35,
Community activist and volunteer

Choloma, Honduras

This is Lopez Arellano.
This is my neighborhood.

Long before I was born,
the people who founded
this community all came
from somewhere else.

The land where they
came from was wanted by
people who had lots of
money, so they used military
force to take that land.
The people were displaced.

So, when they arrived here,
they basically had nothing.

And in some ways not
much has changed since.

Sometimes we have electricity,
sometimes there are cuts.
Water is even more scarce, because
some communities get water
once in 15 or 20 days. Public services
are almost non-existent.

And then there's
the crime. Choloma
has one of the
highest femicide
rates in the country.

Part of the volunteer job I do for
different organizations is to
go around with authorities and
collect the bodies of women.

The *maras* and the
pandillas, as they're
known, extort people
for a "war tax." They
sexually exploit women.
They tell children from
10, 12, 13 years of age
that they need to join the
gang or they will be
dismembered. That is how
they recruit children.

I myself have been threatened several times.

I tell my husband that if I don't make it home one day to tell our children I love them and that I died doing what I believe in. If I die, I know someone else will be there to continue with my legacy.

You learn to deal with the fear.

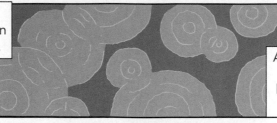

Yes, there are a lot of problems in my community.

And that was before *two* catastrophic hurricanes hit us in *two* weeks.

Hurricane Eta. November 6, 2020.

Climate change has been bringing more extreme storms to Honduras in recent years, but nothing prepared us for this.

I'm a volunteer on the local emergency team CODEL. I received some training. But nothing prepared me for what was coming. The country was not prepared for it.

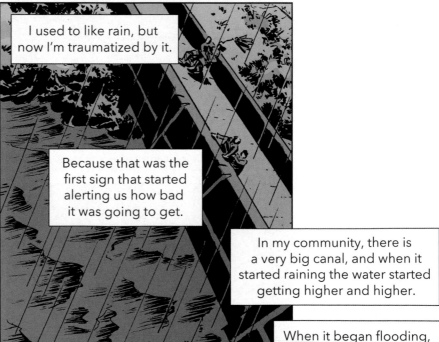

I used to like rain, but now I'm traumatized by it.

Because that was the first sign that started alerting us how bad it was going to get.

In my community, there is a very big canal, and when it started raining the water started getting higher and higher.

When it began flooding, it sounded like a lion.

The sound of water was so frightening that people started using ropes. They started pulling up their beds, their fridges, their tables, so the water wouldn't reach their things.

The ones hit the hardest were of course the ones at the lowest level of the community.

By 10:30 p.m., the river had already overflowed. And at that exact moment there was very heavy wind.

That's when I started panicking.

I asked God, "Why is this happening right now? How are we going to deal with this?"

A community member told me, "Come on, get up, we need to help people who need to evacuate!"

We kept asking churches to open their doors so they could use it as a refuge, until we found some that would.

The rains lasted from 10:30 at night until six in the morning.

There was no break from the criminals.

Some of them stayed behind and asked for payoffs to take care of the houses that were left unattended.

The interesting part of it that wasn't captured by any media, is the fact that the hurricane forced some gang members into the territories of rivals.

Boom
Booom
Boooom

The *maras* and the *pandillas* would identify each other by means of fireworks and the different sounds that they made.

That way they could recognize whether friends or foes were in the area. Or if the police arrived.

While I was trying to help others, someone told me my sister was missing. I was afraid that my sister was probably drowning because it was lower where she lived*.

I asked someone who had a jet ski to take me to where my sister lived. I couldn't even recognize the streets because they were completely flooded. I could only see some of the roofs of the houses.

*I found my sister. My house became a refuge for my sister and other neighbors.

We hit something under the water. The man asked me to check what it was.

It was the head of a little boy.

All these months later and I still haven't processed what I witnessed.

We rescued a young woman. She was clinging to a tree.

She told me she had been holding her baby in her arms. But she fell asleep and the baby dropped into the river, where the current took him away.

We couldn't rescue everyone, but I'm grateful for those we could.

Nobody was prepared for a second hurricane, so even though it wasn't as strong as the first one, in some ways it hit harder.

Hurricane Iota. November 18, 2020.

The people in my community were already isolated for two weeks when the second hurricane hit.

We had the help of a volunteer Santa during Christmas that visited one of the shelters. And when he was there, there was a little boy, who was very enthusiastic to see him.

Santa gave him lots of presents, but the kid was keeping the presents for his grandfather.

Nobody had the guts to tell the boy that his grandfather had died during the floods.

This devastated community is my home.

After my mother abandoned me, my paternal grandmother raised me here. There were ten of us in a small house and we had very little.

As a little girl, I would go to the market to sell chocolates and aprons with my grandmother.

And one day, I saw them. These women demanding basic rights for our community.

I remember them going through the streets with pans and spoons and making lots of noise, even burning tires, so that attention would be paid to the needs of the community. I can recall all of these events.

That was the first time I learned about volunteering.

And I knew what I wanted to do with my life. I wanted to make my grandmother proud.

That is why I keep doing what I do. Trying to make life better for the people of my community.

There are still families that don't have a proper house. They lost everything.

The community is still very vulnerable to floods. I'm afraid especially as we're starting the rainy season this year.

I worry that there will be more of these storms as climate change gets worse.

CHAPTER 3
THE POLAR BEARS ON DANGEROUSLY THIN ICE

**Alysa McCall, 34,
Director of Conservation Outreach
at Polar Bears International**

As a polar bear scientist, the best time of the year for me is during the polar bear migration near Churchill, Manitoba.

It's a congregation of bears that allows us this firsthand view that we don't really get anywhere else in the world.

So polar bear scientists like me all flock to Churchill — along with the tourists and tour operators.

Here, every fall we simply get to watch polar bears be polar bears, up close and for weeks on end.

It's the best place in the world to study the polar bear migration.

**Churchill,
Manitoba, Canada**

There are no fences or boundaries or anything. So, bears are coming in and out of this one small area on the coast. The bears that stick around are sometimes quite curious — they'll come right up to the buggy, put their paws on the vehicle. You can come up nose-to-nose with a polar bear. They could jump up if they really wanted to.

We're quite safe on the buggy, and it lets us study these animals *really* closely.

The polar bears in that region and across Hudson Bay are forced onto land when the ice melts in the summer.

And then every fall when the ice freezes up, they leave to go back on the bay in search of seals.

But during this transitional period, as the weather gets colder in the early fall, they start moving towards the coast near Churchill to wait for the ice to return.

Every year, bear season lasts about four to eight weeks. And as soon as the ice freezes on the bay, they are gone.

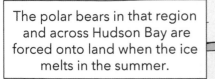

But that timeline is changing. We are noticing increases in the amount of time these polar bears are spending on land.

Because of our ability to get there, these are the best studied polar bears in the world.

December 2021

I went on maternity leave, then the pandemic came, so I skipped a couple of years. This year, I came back to see that the ice is quite late. The bears usually leave around mid-November.

There are bears still here – and it's early December. They haven't eaten since June when the ice broke up. These are hungry polar bears.

Because of the amazing data set that we have on Hudson Bay, we can see how these polar bears are affected by those changes.

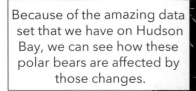

These were the first polar bears in the world that we could show were affected by changes in the sea ice happening due to climate change.

We call them "the big fat hairy white canaries in the coal mines."

A lot of what we know is from physical mark-recapture work that's both dangerous and expensive.

That involves going up in a helicopter and looking for a polar bear. And when you see one that's appropriate in a safe area, you can tranquilize them with a dart.

I don't do the actual shooting. That's handled by someone much more experienced with guns and special training. In fact, while they're doing the darting, they will often drop me off on the ice or land to lessen weight in the helicopter and make it more maneuverable.

Being all alone on the ice waiting for their return is always interesting. They do leave me with a GPS, radio, warm gear, and a shotgun though... just in case.

After we think the bear is sleeping we land the helicopter, walk up to the bear, and make extra sure it's sleeping.

We check to see if the bear has ear tags and/or a lip tattoo with their individual number. This tells us if the bear is a new capture or recapture. If it is a new capture, we give the bear ear tags and a lip tattoo with its own individual number and record it.
If it's a recapture, we simply note the bear's ID and look it up in our "polar bear bible," a giant binder we bring into the field.

Then we take all sorts of measurements, take a tiny sample of fat from the fatty bum, some hair, a small shaving of claw, and occasionally a vial of blood. These samples are hugely helpful in understanding how the bear is doing health-wise and how it interacts with the environment.

Every time I see one of these animals up close, there's a feeling of awe.

One of the biggest bears that I ever handled weighed close to 1,700 pounds. They are the biggest bears on the planet because of their diet of blubber.

It's hard not to appreciate how this amazing species can survive in one of the most horrible environments I can imagine.

And that environment seems to be getting more dangerous because of climate change.

We are seeing moms have a harder time getting pregnant, staying pregnant and having healthy cubs. This used to be a population that was well-known for triplets, and now triplets are quite rare.

This population also used to be able to wean their cubs earlier than anywhere else in the world because the hunting conditions were so good...

...but now that doesn't happen. These bears are getting smaller.

They're smaller than they were in the 1980s because they're not getting as much food. They're on land longer than they should be, so they're getting more food stressed.

We know they lose about a kilogram of fat a day when they're on land, and that adds up really fast. So we are seeing all these changes over time.

Polar bears do rely on sea ice as a platform to reach their seal prey. They can rarely outswim seals in the water. And they can't rely on terrestrial food sources, which don't have enough calories.

So, the less access to ice they have, the less access to food they have.

And climate change is having an impact on the seals, too.

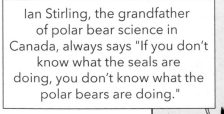

Ian Stirling, the grandfather of polar bear science in Canada, always says "If you don't know what the seals are doing, you don't know what the polar bears are doing."

As it's getting warmer and raining more in the Arctic, we know there've been incidents of layer collapse of the ridges where the seals shelter their babies. We're losing some seals that way.

Killer whales also now have more opportunities to come up north because there is less ice. These poor seals are not used to being preyed on from the sea. And that could eventually mean fewer seals for the polar bears.

We know these bears are on land now three to four weeks longer than they used to be. We see that play out in how often these bears come into town.

It's always been a way of life in Churchill.

You don't go out at night by yourself. You take a cab, or you go with friends and you make noise. You're always scanning around corners and under cars.

But we're now seeing polar bears along the Ontario coast in communities that didn't see them before.

The organization I work for, Polar Bears International, is helping provide supplies, deterrents, and training for affected communities as needed – from bear spray to polar bear safety coloring books for kids.

These bears are looking for food, but they're built to eat blubber, not a terrestrial diet.

In 2017, video of a starving bear taken for National Geographic went viral. That footage was quite something.

We don't know for sure that it's a direct result of loss of food sources connected to climate change. That bear could have been the victim of disease or broken teeth or old age.

I can't say anything about that particular bear, but I can say if the world continues to warm and we do continue to lose ice at that rate, we are going to lose polar bears through starvation events. And *that* is what starvation looks like.

I do wonder.

I'm pretty sure we'll have polar bears into the end of the century. But when my daughter's my age, what is her world going to look like?

Will these polar bears be even more of an exotic animal when she's older? I think about her future every day.

In Western Hudson Bay, the bears largely departed onto the ice between the 3rd and the 10th of December, so we would estimate that freeze-up occurred within the first week of December.

This is approximately two to three weeks later than the average freeze-up date for Hudson Bay. We know males can go a maximum of roughly 180 days without eating. This is cutting it too close.

When we talk about how climate change is impacting polar bears, and it is, we can get some push back because they're not on the brink of extinction. But there are 23,000 to 26,000 of them across the entire Arctic. They're not a high-density species, they reproduce slowly, and their habitat is changing rapidly.

We do know we don't need to lose them. We do have time to protect them.

CHAPTER 4
DROUGHT BRINGS TEARS IN NAMIBIA

Taimi Amutse, 30, Regional Officer for the Namibia Red Cross Society, Omusati region

Since I was a child, I have had a strong desire to help people. I always wanted to be a voice for the most vulnerable members of my community.

Being a humanitarian at the Namibia Red Cross Society has given me the opportunity to make a difference in society by assisting the needy.

Etunda Village, Namibia

Summer 2021

Basically, I coordinate regional activities and ensure the implementation of projects in the Omusati region. I've been providing aid to Angolan refugees who arrived here in the beginning of March.

The camp is on the grounds of a Lutheran church, and has been used for local emergencies like floods. So when the Angolans came, the church let us use it.

The Etunda camp has 2,425 migrants, most of them children, more than 1,400 of them. There are about 600 to 700 women and about 300 men.

They came across the border because they were desperate.

Angola hasn't had rain in nearly three years, resulting in a severe drought and animal losses.

The worst drought in the last 40 years and rising food prices have resulted in highly acute food insecurity in the Cunene, Huila, and Namibe provinces of southwestern Angola. The poor harvests have severely affected people's access to food in this region, which is dependent on agriculture and has led to widespread malnutrition.

This crisis endangered an estimated 1.58 million Angolans by March of 2022.

Some people were telling me their story. They have lost everything. They really worked hard as farmers to provide for their families, but at the end of the day, there was really nothing left for them to feed their families.

And they left their homeland to come to a country where the majority of them had never been before just because of a drought, seeking help and seeking food.

For a person who cares about humanity, it's really quite overwhelming. Quite heartbreaking.

It's the first time going this long without rain, so I think it's due to climate change. Which means the situation will likely continue to get worse.

Due to the drought, these people walked for about five days, covering nearly 150 kilometers (93.2 miles) before arriving in Namibia.

There was really nothing to eat. They would go days and days without eating anything.

They were saying that their journey became long and difficult and those who became weak or tired along the way, they were actually left behind.

Some children died on the way.

As a result of this, the majority of them, in particular pregnant women and a lot of children, were actually in a very horrible condition when they arrived in Namibia. They had major health issues.

So it was really quite an overwhelming experience to be there.

The children were malnourished. They had scabies. They had diarrhea and were vomiting.

Even when they arrived at the camp, we couldn't save everyone. There were children who passed away at the camp because they were really, really malnourished.

Mwatjakatana Thofua was one of the women at the camp who lost her 6-month-old. She was traumatized and devastated about her loss.

She kept muttering to herself, "God, what have we done to deserve this? I traveled from my own country to lose my child in this country, and there is nothing I could do to save her."

It was heartbreaking to watch her grieve while also trying to be strong for her other four children.

One thing Mwatjakatana said that stuck with me was that "this too shall pass," that "nothing lasts forever." I was moved by the strength of this woman.

At first, yeah, it was overwhelming to witness how climate change could cause such ecological destruction that would force so many to abandon their ways of life.

But later on, I just started getting used to the whole situation. They were having their babies. They were going on.

I wanted to bring them comfort, but several comforted *me.*

There was this man called Fernando, who was maybe 19 or 20. He was one of the happiest guys that I'd ever seen. He didn't really let the whole situation get to him. He very much still had hope that things were going to get better and he was going to get home to his family again.

For me that mindset was really just amazing.

The women cooked for their families because there were actually households in the camp. Then some would do laundry, wash their clothes. And then they didn't really have much else to do. There were some that would leave the camps to look for jobs nearby.

The kids adapted. They were really boisterous. They played in a new environment.

When they got here in Namibia, a lot of them were just recovering from being malnourished. Some were active, running around the camp and playing, but the majority of them were still recovering from their ordeal.

Because this crisis is happening during a pandemic, it could have been much worse.

Only one Covid-19 case was reported in the camp: a child who died at the age of 3. The family in the camp was screened for Covid-19, and fortunately no one tested positive.

My job included registering the Angolans who came. I also coordinated the activities of the camp, the distribution of donations that came in, and handing out food together with the volunteers. I was also engaging with various stakeholders in the region to ensure effective implementation of the project.

Malnutrition, scabies, diarrhea, and vomiting were the bigger problems in the camp.

Every day was very special to me. The Angolans were some of the kindest people I've ever seen. Every time they saw us, they were really just eager to talk to us and then share some love with them.

They were really grateful. Every day they were like, "Thank you so much for being here. We really do appreciate it. We will never forget you."

I will never forget them, either.

The emergency camp was officially closed on Jan. 6, 2022, when the migrants were repatriated to Angola.

Growing up I always just wanted to help the needy. Make a difference in society. So, this work is actually a dream come true for me.

But climate change is impacting the world right now. Things are changing right here in Namibia.

My country is truly a sunny place, with 300 days of sunshine on average per year. Summer runs from October to April and temperatures can reach 40 degrees Celsius (104° Fahrenheit) which fall at night to cool levels. It's getting hotter.

Drought and floods have been the most visible manifestations of climate change in Namibia, affecting water availability, food production and people's livelihoods, because the majority of Namibians are communal farmers who rely on staple crops and their livestock for a living.

There will be more people who need help, and I will be here to do what I can.

CHAPTER 5
SHINING A SPOTLIGHT ON THE BLIGHT OF CHINESE POWER PLANTS

My struggle as a photographer is, how do you make the scope of climate change tangible?

Ian Teh, 51, Malaysia-based documentary photographer

We're just not designed as a species to think long term over vast amounts of time, or of the generations of people who will succeed us. Our brains are designed to address dangers on the immediate horizon.

Like in China. When I started shooting coal plants, China was building two power stations per week to meet energy demand. It was a record.

Today, that record is still getting broken, but most of it's not in China. A lot of that is shifting into poorer countries. That technology is being exported to other countries, because these poorer countries have an immediate need for electricity.

So my work is almost about showing the immediacy of how we need to fix this problem right now.

In reality, what's happening is that we're sacrificing so much from the future, that when it does come time to pay, God knows what that cost is going to be.

What do I hope my photography will accomplish? I think a change of behavior would obviously be great, but I think the first thing is opening eyes.

I was very interested in being an illustrator as a teenager. But my art teacher actually told me that they're going to want to see more than just beautiful drawings in art college. I would need to show a curious mind and try a range of other mediums. So I tried my hand at photography using my dad's camera.

And I realized when I was shooting that I got kind of interested in photography. I was amazed by how the camera translated the world.

But my big education in photography came from winning a prize in my second year in college in the U.K. I asked them to hold back on the winnings – a travel prize and a fancy camera – until I graduated.

I then chose to go to China afterwards to travel and explore my roots. I also really wanted to be in a country where I could barely speak the language. Because from the books I'd read on photographers that I admired, they seemed to be pretty solitary in the way they worked.

I also grew up watching the '89 Tiananmen Square massacre, and documentaries coming out of China as the country was slowly opening up under Deng Xiaoping's reign. That really got me interested in what was going on over there.

I intended to travel for two months. I ended up backpacking through China and Southeast Asia for six months. But I kept coming back to China. I was literally saving up all the cash I had from waiting jobs and then just heading back out again to keep building my portfolio.

My first big professional credit that got published was with The Independent magazine in the U.K. in 1999, a story that I went over to China to cover — the construction of the Three Gorges Dam.

My main focus of the dam was not so much the dam itself, but the impact it was having on the communities that were living behind it. An area that stretched over 435 miles (700 kilometers) and affected close to 1.5 million people.

The Chinese government actually had to remove all these cities that were in that region. Literally disassemble them and rebuild new settlements on higher ground or in other places.

I wasn't prepared for what I saw.

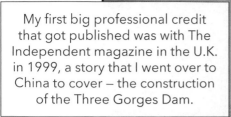

I traveled up the river and would disembark and then see cities just decimated … like it was a war zone. And then you have people still inside who were trying to go about living their life.

One striking image I remember photographing was this barber. I was across the street watching this guy cutting a customer's hair in a building that was reduced to rubble.

The government was trying to resettle these people, but if you get resettled in a new town too early, there's no one there to whom you can sell your craft or goods. So you had this kind of like limbo period, where people tried to stay as long as possible to keep working.

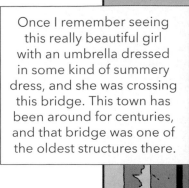

Once I remember seeing this really beautiful girl with an umbrella dressed in some kind of summery dress, and she was crossing this bridge. This town has been around for centuries, and that bridge was one of the oldest structures there.

About a week later that bridge was dynamited.

I photographed that series from 1999 through 2003. Because after that first trip, I just decided, this is something huge that's happening.

Building my craft took me across China, and to places like Cuba and the favelas of Brazil. But I think in all those travels, I felt like I was struggling with certain types of human stories.

Like if people were obviously suffering greatly, and at the same time, I was making a living by trying to tell their story. There was a conflict of motivation going on inside me in my mid-20s. I was trying to find my moral compass, as well as the kind of stories I wanted to cover.

I ended up deciding that I would like to focus more on environmental stories.

That was when I had some kind of epiphany, realizing that the change that was going on in China was so great and so fast that I should keep coming back.

Around 2006, I started researching and looking into China's coal industry, because it was so massive. Miners were having lots of accidents. At that time, it was the world's most dangerous job. I think 80 percent of accidents in the industry globally were happening in China.

At the same time, you know, you'd have cities just sprouting up even more skyscrapers, so they were doubling in size all along the eastern seaboard of China. That led to an insatiable demand for burning coal.

I initially went to Shanxi province, which is in the northeast of China, to this town called Datong, the coal capital of China.

I didn't even have to go to the most polluted city to experience the effects. The acrid smell of burning coal would hit me as I entered the international airport terminal in Beijing from my flight. The heating in China was state-controlled and individual building compounds would burn coal to heat water and pipe it to homes.

This had the compound effect of tainting the air with fumes from burning coal throughout the city. When I traveled to these mining towns, though, the level of pollution was even greater.

I remember back in the late '90s, one resident said to me, "Oh, you're going to Datong, that's where it rains 'black rain.'" That stayed with me. Years later, when I decided to work on the coal industry, that memory made Datong the first place I chose to visit.

I went there in 2006 to start shooting this place, where these miners were working in coking plants (where cooking coal is made from metallurgical coal in furnaces).

I wrote the following about the bus ride from Linfen to the Yellow River: "The dust is everywhere, you can feel it on your fingers as something abrasive and dry that you would like to rub away but never can. It coats every surface — from leaves and crops to the buildings and factories lining both sides of the road."

I spoke to a resident that I knew who used to be a truck driver and he said to me, "Our government has exported all our blue skies to the West."

That became the inspiration for my series on the coal industry that I shot from 2006 to 2009 called "Dark Clouds." I was looking at how the worker was essentially a cog in a much larger machine.

And while the state was pursuing its national dream, these workers were also pursuing their own individualized dreams. Because here was an opportunity where they could leave their farmlands, in droves, often to work in dangerous jobs for more money.

At that point, I had another epiphany. It suddenly struck me that what was happening in China was not just China's problem necessarily.

Yes, China had agency in deciding how they were going to actually develop the country. But this was a much bigger problem you could trace back centuries, right back to the British Industrial Revolution.

Victorians started industrializing and became rich that way, creating a template that has existed since that time. The process just got more powerful and more efficient over time.

That template for economic growth moves around every time. Essentially, carbon emissions are exported to different parts of the world, usually developing nations because that's where it's cheapest and the environmental rules are most lax.

Once a country becomes a middle-class society, residents are perhaps less accepting of what they willingly allowed two decades earlier.

So this was what was happening in China, but on a scale that no one could imagine, because this was a country with 1.2 billion people.

China's lifted some 800 million people from the poverty line during that period. It's worth reflecting on the trade-off with the carbon emissions produced throughout that process. Now imagine how this has been replicated throughout time for every other wealthy industrialized nation today.

Because there's always a trade-off in terms of countries wanting to grow economically, and what they're willing to sacrifice in order to do that.

My most recent assignment was in March 2020 in Jakarta just before the shutdown, which is one of the fastest sinking cities in the world.

In Asian cities with the fastest subsidence, highly populated and industrialized areas sink faster. The cause: excessive groundwater extraction. It depletes the underground aquifers causing the land to compact under the weight of the city. At the same time, rising sea levels will hasten the problem of flooding. It's a problem other coastal cities will face in the coming years.

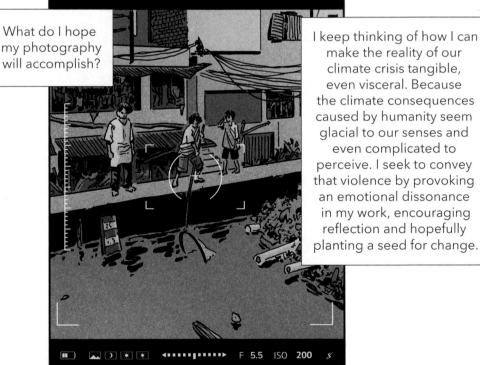

What do I hope my photography will accomplish?

I keep thinking of how I can make the reality of our climate crisis tangible, even visceral. Because the climate consequences caused by humanity seem glacial to our senses and even complicated to perceive. I seek to convey that violence by provoking an emotional dissonance in my work, encouraging reflection and hopefully planting a seed for change.

How do I open eyes and minds?

CHAPTER 6
RACING AGAINST TIME TO SAVE THE KOALAS

Most of the 50 or so people who volunteer at Friends of the Koala have a great affection for all of our wildlife.

Lismore, New South Wales, Australia

But we put most of our time and energy into koalas. Because we know if we can save koalas — and I have my doubts about that — we would save a lot of other wildlife that share the same habitat.

Because the key to saving wildlife is saving that habitat.

Australians love koalas because they're cute-looking and are part of our precious wildlife that is in real trouble.

Koalas have recently had their status at both the state and Commonwealth level raised to "endangered." So most of us want to try to save these animals.

Then came the bushfires that burned from November 2019 to February 2020.

We honestly did not come to terms with the fact that we were in an area where parts of it could burn. Because in the northern part of the region there are rainforests. Usually rainforests don't get burnt.

This time, they did.

The worst bushfire in the area was down around Ballina, which became a pitch fire.

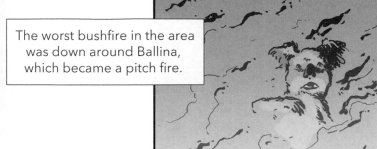

Once a fire starts, it burns underground and just keeps going on and on. And no matter how much water is put on it, the fire just keeps burning. So there was quite a lot of devastation down there.

It was a particularly bad fire. Fifty percent of the land mass burned.

And we know in that area alone we lost about 2,000 koalas. So for us that was a devastating impact.

On one call during the bushfires, my partner Bill and I went out to a rural property to rescue a koala. You could see that it had been previously forested with koala food trees. And all of that had been burned down.

The people who called us had tried to save their house and they saved a shed. They were worried about this koala sitting on the ground.

They asked if it was going to be all right. But we had no idea until we could get it to a vet.

And as it so happened, while it hadn't been burned by the fire itself, the radiation had actually baked its insides, so it had to be euthanized.

One day during the fires we were called to a rescue out past Red Hill (about a five-hour drive from Lismore).

That was very scary because it was actually still burning quite badly on both sides of the road. We arrived to find this female with a joey on her back on the only tree left standing.

We actually got her down because luckily the fire service had a cherry picker there.

They turned out to be fine. That was a real delight because generally when we're rescuing koalas from fires, if they weren't dead by the time they got to the care center, they were euthanized.

We named them Flame and Spirit. Those names just seemed appropriate.

This is Ember. She was the last of the koalas to be rescued from the bushfires.

She came in singed, her paws had been burned badly, and her claws bent upward instead of down after being disfigured by the intense heat.

We didn't know if she was going to be able to climb a tree ever again.

She was in the hospital for several months, but then she came back and was admitted to the care center. Then she came out to the sanctuary to practice climbing because her claws were so badly damaged.

She spent quite a bit of time with us in our rehabilitation center before she was released. She went up and down. We have 50 trees in our "kindy," as we call it, and she just went up all of them. She loved it.

Ember came back to visit a year and a half after we released her. She's had one joey, and we think she's got another one on the way now. It's as if she wants to introduce her baby to us.

This area is her range now. We could not take her back to where we rescued her, because none of the habitat is still there. It's all pretty much gone because of the fire.

In the end, we rescued 21 koalas, but were only able to release seven. The others were too far gone.

But you do this for the ones you can save.

It's a really joyful feeling to release a recovered koala back into the wild. When you go out and open the cage, and they just bolt up a tree.

We had a release just a few weeks ago. She came out of that cage just like a rocket.

She went straight up the tree, stopped briefly to look back at us, and then off she went. It's a lovely feeling.

Koalas are beloved in Australia now, but they weren't protected for much of this country's history.

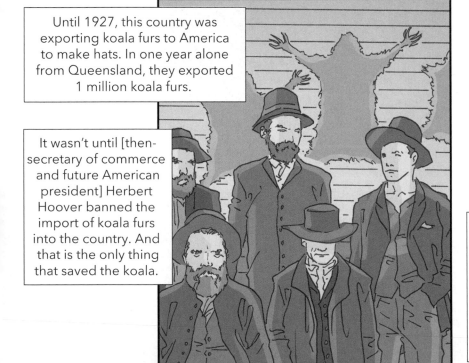

Until 1927, this country was exporting koala furs to America to make hats. In one year alone from Queensland, they exported 1 million koala furs.

It wasn't until [then-secretary of commerce and future American president] Herbert Hoover banned the import of koala furs into the country. And that is the only thing that saved the koala.

There were millions when white people arrived here, and to think that it's down to a maximum of 120,000 left — that really indicates the size of the problem.

How did I get involved? I was a lecturer at Southern Cross University, a former mayor of Lismore, and a member of the local council for 18 years. Back when I was on the council, a friend of mine, the then president of Friends of the Koala, convinced me to help draft a planned koala management program for the area.

I retired from the uni in 2009. A year later, I started doing work initially with Friends of the Koala. It all went from there. Bill and I now have koalas living on our property.

They're just beautiful animals, and if I can do something to help them, it's a beautiful feeling.

They need a lot of help.

Only recently did we come to understand what was happening in terms of climate change. Between 2017 and 2019 we had the two driest years, the longest dry period on record in this part of the country –

– which was most unusual because usually this is one of the wettest areas in New South Wales and in Australia.

During that two-year drought we found we were taking in far more koalas.

We would get a report from someone in the community that there is a koala just sitting at the bottom of a tree. It's just sitting there; it's not doing anything.

And when you pick it up and take it in, what had happened was the animal was dehydrated to the stage where its organs started breaking down, so they had to be euthanized.

This is the direct result of the trees having lost their moisture. Because koalas, unlike most animals, get most of their water from the leaves. And these trees were really dry.

So when the fires came, their impact was even more significant because the rainforests burned.

Koalas have recently had their status at both state and Commonwealth levels raised to endangered. Australia has a shocking record in regard to extinction of our wildlife – one of the worst in the world.

It's only going to get worse as climate change makes their habitat even hotter and drier.

That's the biggest worry going forward. Until it's protected, and neither the federal nor state government protects koala habitats, we will just continue to move toward that tipping point. Once they start sliding down you can't retrieve them. It's a one way ticket to extinction.

That's why we do all we can to save them.

CHAPTER 7
DESPERATE RESCUES ON THE HIGH SEAS

Marseilles France, December 2021

The mission of this ship is to rescue people from distress at sea and provide emergency medical treatment on board. To protect survivors on board and testify about the situation witnessed at sea.

These are migrants who, in a desperate attempt to flee Libya, have no other alternatives other than sailing on vessels that are unfit for the sea.

The Ocean Viking is charted by the SOS MEDITERRANEE, which I work for, and operated in partnership with the International Federation of Red Cross and Red Crescent Societies (IFRC).

SOS MEDITERRANEE is a European maritime and humanitarian organization for the rescue of life on the Mediterranean. It was founded by citizens in May 2015 in response to the deaths in those waters – and the failure of the European Union to prevent those deaths.

Olivier, 43, logistician, SOS MEDITERRANEE

I witnessed my first rescue on Dec. 16, 2021. The arrival of the people on board was an unforgettable moment. As I expected, after seeing so many images in the media, they were mostly shoeless with just trousers and a T-shirt on their backs.

But what I couldn't imagine was the sheer volume of emotion that came out at that moment. These people had just escaped a foretold death, a culmination of years of suffering.

I took a long journey to be on this boat. I live in Italy, so I studied philosophy. And then right after that, while I was doing a Ph.D., I started working in refugee camps in Italy. That became my life's calling.

Francesco Fornari, 34, IFRC post rescue coordinator

I have done three missions on the Ocean Viking as post-rescue team leader. Because basically, this ship is like a floating refugee camp.* So, you do the exact job you normally do on shore.

*The term "refugee" is a specific legal criteria that is not technically met in the situation of these rescues.

I am a family physician with a background in public health and anthropology. I have a full-time job with the Red Cross as a rapid response manager. So, I am on standby at home in Montreal for an alert to leave to wherever in the world I'm needed.

I've worked with the Red Cross since 2012. I am part of the teams that respond to disasters, conflicts and public health emergencies, such as dengue or Ebola outbreaks, to work with local and international health responders and teams.

Every once in a while, I also deploy as a physician, as was the case during my deployment on the Ocean Viking. I was there to help treat the survivors once they were rescued from the water.

Maria Munoz-Bertrand, 53, IFRC rapid response manager and physician

After a period of training in Marseille, we set sail, heading between the Italian coast and Corsica and Sardinia, and then down through the Strait between Italy and Sicily, and then toward the coast of Libya, staying always in international waters.

We patrol in international waters, searching for boats in distress.

There are these overcrowded boats desperate enough to try to flee the coast of Libya.

They have to be desperate to attempt this journey. Because the boats are not seaworthy. These boats are about 33 to 39 feet long, about 10 feet wide, and usually jammed with 130 or 140 people.

On the last patrol, there were two people who died before we could rescue them. Because their boat was taking in water and they were in the middle when they slipped. They ended up belly down and drowned in water that was full of gasoline, vomit, and fecal matter.

Why do they undertake such a dangerous journey? People flee their country of origin for a myriad of different and complex reasons. People are fleeing because of war, famine, poverty, conflicts, forced marriages and many more reasons.

Some survivors told us that they could no longer provide for their family in their country of origin because of floods or droughts devastating their crops and other means to live. In the hope of finding opportunities to keep providing for their family, some told us that they did not have other choices.

It's weird, because you almost never meet a person whose escape is a direct process. Say someone lives in Mali and there is a drought or their farm got decertified. So, they leave to go to Libya and try to find a job.

But then they are arrested. The police call their family for blackmail, they send money, and now the person is in debt to their family. So, they decide to go to Europe to pay off this debt. This happens.

The reason they are going to ask for political asylum in Italy may be because of what happened in Libya. But the reason why it started in Libya is because there was a drought in Mali. There's never just one straight answer.

There are mostly two kinds of boats that the rescuers see. There are rubber boats, and the experience of the search and rescue team is that these are very cheap boats made of very thin rubber and filled way beyond their capacity. People are really literally touching up against one another on all sides. You can find 100 people or more in such a boat that should not sail far from shore with more than a few people.

Then there are the wooden boats that are typically very old. People on board can fall into the water very easily. And if you spend more than an hour in the sea, you will likely die from hypothermia. So if people fall in the water, the chance of actually getting them out and saving them is very slim.

Even though we know there are boats in the area, finding them isn't easy. We have people on watch on the bridge, with binoculars. The radar is useless because these boats are something like 20 inches above the water. So, any wave could look like a boat on the screen.

There is a 1-800 hotline number that survivors on boats can call and give their position. Sometimes people will travel with cellphones, so they call this number for help.

There are also planes that go over the sea and try to spot boats in distress and let rescue ships in the area know their location. The Ocean Viking is not the only boat in the area. There are at least seven or eight other organizations.

That's how the specific rescue I witnessed happened: Someone called the hotline and gave their position.

**Dec. 16, 2021
Off the coast of Libya**

We had all these drills for everything, including the search and rescue drill. After the search and rescue coordinator spent most of the night looking for a boat, the team was woken up around 5 a.m. and we were ready.

We could actually see the boat from where we were in the darkness of night — it was only a shadow that was a bit darker than the sea.

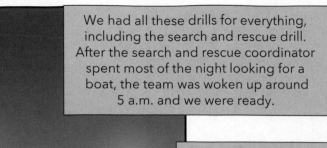

The SOS MEDITERRANEE rescue team launched two RHIBs*. And they approached the boat from both the stern and from the bow, turning around and approaching at the same time. That's so the people on board don't suddenly overload one side and capsize the boat.

*Rigid-Hulled Inflatable Boats.

Both of the RHIBs calmly talked to the survivors in the boat in English and in Arabic, and then start giving life vests to each person on board.

From the boat, we could see the black shape suddenly become orange in the darkness after the rescue team had handed out the life vests. You could see a wall of orange because their boat was so overloaded. But the search and rescue technique was so professional that it was done safely in no time.

Once that's done, they do shuttle runs back to the Ocean Viking, filling the RHIBs with people.

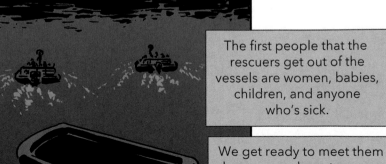

The first people that the rescuers get out of the vessels are women, babies, children, and anyone who's sick.

We get ready to meet them because we have to assess each survivor quickly to see if they need any specific care or support.

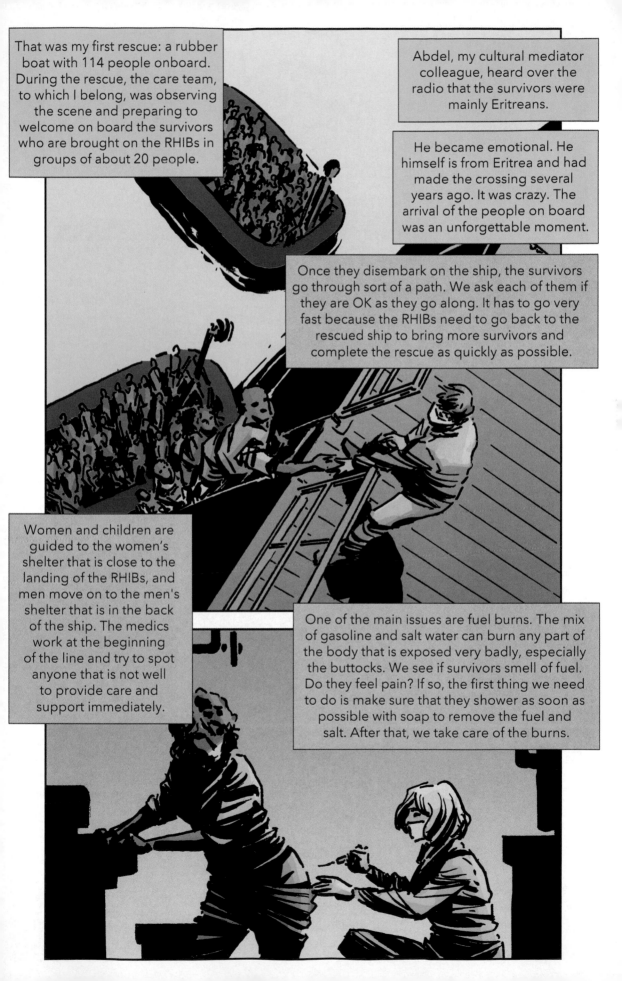

That was my first rescue: a rubber boat with 114 people onboard. During the rescue, the care team, to which I belong, was observing the scene and preparing to welcome on board the survivors who are brought on the RHIBs in groups of about 20 people.

Abdel, my cultural mediator colleague, heard over the radio that the survivors were mainly Eritreans.

He became emotional. He himself is from Eritrea and had made the crossing several years ago. It was crazy. The arrival of the people on board was an unforgettable moment.

Once they disembark on the ship, the survivors go through sort of a path. We ask each of them if they are OK as they go along. It has to go very fast because the RHIBs need to go back to the rescued ship to bring more survivors and complete the rescue as quickly as possible.

Women and children are guided to the women's shelter that is close to the landing of the RHIBs, and men move on to the men's shelter that is in the back of the ship. The medics work at the beginning of the line and try to spot anyone that is not well to provide care and support immediately.

One of the main issues are fuel burns. The mix of gasoline and salt water can burn any part of the body that is exposed very badly, especially the buttocks. We see if survivors smell of fuel. Do they feel pain? If so, the first thing we need to do is make sure that they shower as soon as possible with soap to remove the fuel and salt. After that, we take care of the burns.

There were two newborns. Both of them looked like they had suffered from intrauterine growth retardation. That can happen when the mother has either not been fed enough or is very stressed during pregnancy, which was probably the case for the mothers in Libya.

We also worry about dehydration and diseases like scabies, which is a disease that happens in poor, overcrowded and unhygienic places. We couldn't really check for nutrition with the equipment we had, but we could check hemoglobin levels, and found anemic people on board.

And then there were a lot of people suffering from mental health issues, due to stress and the terrible situations they endured during their journey.

My daily routine is waking up early and going on the deck after 6, 7. I get dressed in coveralls and a mask to avoid potentially getting infected on the deck. I say hello to everyone helping distribute breakfast. I stay with the survivors, talk to them.

I talk to people from the medical team to know if there is something to signal or something worrisome. Talking to people from the care team, I spend a lot of time with the control mediator to understand who people are and where they're coming from. We try to map out the families so that when they disembark, they don't get separated.

I try to stay on deck as much as possible. Like seven, eight hours a day. Then around 5 p.m., we distribute dinner. You make sure that they are warm and safe. And then around 9 p.m., we go to sleep. It's not really fun.

You do whatever you can to lighten the boredom...including playing with the children.

Their day usually starts with breakfast. Our teams prepare tea and food for survivors onboard the Ocean Viking and then supervises the distribution.

Throughout the day, we organize activities, which vary according to the number of survivors, weather conditions and the needs that are identified. Some examples: Games are distributed, musical instruments are given out, clothes are washed, a hairdresser's salon is organized, and mobile phones are charged. These activities might seem trivial, but reveal to be important on board.

I also regularly go round the stations to ensure that the teams have the items we use and distribute on a daily basis (soap, toothpaste, bin bags, cleaning products, etc.).

We keep on patrolling the same area for some days – and then we sail north towards Malta and Italy. When there are survivors on board, our search and rescue coordinator will send a message to the countries that can grant a port of safety. Basically, it can be Malta or Italy.

So, every day, she would write to the these places and say we have this many survivors on board, please grant us a port of safety for them to disembark.

Countries have been taking a long time to grant those ports of safety to the survivors aboard the Ocean Viking, and to the other rescue boats. So, during that time, the survivors are trapped on board.

There's nothing to do on the boat except worry. Survivors can't communicate with people back home to let them know that they're safe. So they're worried about themselves and the people back home. It's a very difficult time for them.

Every day we would ask for a port of safety, for almost 10 days without success.

But on Dec. 24, the Italian authorities said, "Yes, you can disembark in Trapani, on the western part of Sicily." It was a Christmas gift! And so, we disembarked the survivors on the 25th.

They were all crying when they heard the news because they were huddled on the ship for so very long. It was super crowded, and they were tired.

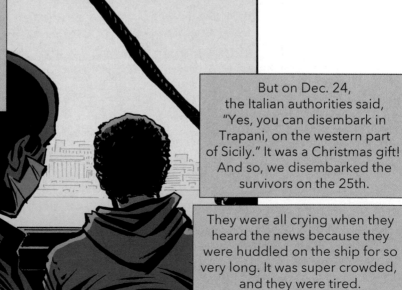

When survivors left the boat, we were really happy, and they were also happy. I think they were very grateful as well. I mean, especially after the experiences they had on shore and the situations they left behind.

There is an undeniable personal satisfaction when they disembark safely. You feel like you did something. But at the same time, there is always a bit of despair in it. Because, then what? They don't have the tools. They don't know the language, nor have the papers to do anything. You hope for the best.

And in the coming years, climate change is going to make the crisis worse. There will be more and more displaced people. I pray I'm not going to be one of them.

I mean, the borders of the livable world are shrinking year by year. It's getting worse and worse and worse. Libya. Ukraine. Syria. Those were all countries where people had been fine just a few years ago. In the meantime, the crew of the Ocean Viking continues to try to help, inspired by international maritime laws and the principle of humanity.

Something that came to my mind during the first patrol is that the wooden deck on which we work and the rescued people live, that wooden deck resembles a stage.

The Ocean Viking is a theater where we play the same tragedy, with different subplots for every patrol. A woman giving birth. A family that reunites. Sadly, you'll have death and sorrow. But the tragedy is articulated around the same topic: the contradiction of a society that has human rights in its constitutional values, and overrides them on a daily basis with its policies.

But being a tragedy doesn't mean being necessarily *tragic*. Happy endings can happen, too.

CHAPTER 8
"YOU'RE LITERALLY LIVING IN AN OVEN"

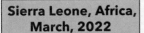

Yvonne Aki-Sawyerr, 54, Mayor of Freetown

Climate change is here. It's real. It's impacting my city today.

Our solutions are not the same solutions as the West. We don't have the industry. When we talk about "net zero" (carbon emissions), we're already at almost zero. Because, you know, we're not emitting.

But we are suffering.

We can feel it. Extreme heat stress is real for us. It's very, very real, and it's getting worse.

For my most vulnerable residents who live in slums, they are living in cookers. Because the affordable housing material of choice for people living in the cities of this country is corrugated iron.

Can you imagine what that feels like? You're literally living in an oven. And the health implications of that are disastrous.

So, our conversation is a *different* conversation. It's about how what we do also affects our local space.

For example, from a health perspective, our fuel sources lead to a lot of respiratory conditions and lung cancer. On a global scale, our emissions are insignificant.

But on a local level, the carbon monoxide from inefficient, fuel-guzzling, dirty diesel still being used here? That's killing people.

We have to find solutions to the effects of climate change that disproportionally affect our region.

We're currently working on introducing a cable car system for mass transport. Do we need to have clean transport? Yes, of course we do. But not because we are part of the global powers that are producing carbon emissions from cars.

Ninety percent of greenhouse gas emissions come from G20 countries. That's not us. But what we do produce is still killing our people.

I never thought running a city of 1.2 million people would be my job.

Though I was born in Freetown, I was working in business, management consulting, and project management in the U.K., where I earned my master's at the London School of Economics.

Long story short, my journey started with me responding to the atrocities of Jan. 6, 1999.* I set up a nonprofit for my home country in my spare time. It's still functional and impactful 22 years later. But not-for-profits can only do so much.

*Editor's note: The day when the guerilla army known as the Revolutionary United Front launched a spree in the city that left thousands murdered, and thousands more mutilated and raped.

I joined my husband in working on private sector investment in Sierra Leone. Property development.

But I was drawn into the public sector during the 2014 Ebola crisis.

When Ebola struck, I could not just watch it on my TV screen. I couldn't.

So, on Nov. 13, 2014, I got on a very empty plane, I flew to Freetown, and within a couple of weeks, I became the director of planning for the National Ebola Response Centre.

I put my hat on as a consultant, and I immediately went to the Sierra Leone team and said, "Look, I'm here. What do you need help with?" They said, "We need beds."

The threads of everything I've done over a number of years were responsible for leading the planning – working with professionals, with technical people along a huge spectrum. I was awarded a gold medal by the president and an OBE by the queen of England.

When that ended, I was asked by the government to lead the post-recovery program. While doing that, I saw firsthand the destruction that was happening to our environment on a local level from deforestation.

About a month after the Ebola crisis was contained, I was driving along a mountain road that goes to a small village called Bathurst, where my husband is originally from. That whole place was protected forest. I've done that drive dozens of times.

And I suddenly stopped and realized that the trees were gone.

I was shocked. I stopped the car and found myself sobbing.

To compound that, I could see the sanitation challenge facing the city. Sanitation has a direct bearing on the environment because of the destruction to the ecosystems. Garbage was being dumped into the mangroves.

There was literally garbage in the waterways, in the canals, in the streams.

On Aug. 14, 2017, 1,000 people died in three minutes when the mountain caved. People were buried alive in the mudslides.

Deforestation contributed to that disaster. Without trees holding the silt in place, the rains washed it downhill, further clogging many drainage systems already clogged by poor sanitation.

All of these problems have consequences.

One of the things I did in my position as the head of the recovery team was going ward by ward and doing a massive cleanup of the city, and trying to set up a system which would then be sustainable. But I also had drone images taken of the mountains.

I cleared the furniture out of a big meeting room at the statehouse. And I just did this dramatic thing where I put before-and-after pictures on the walls for when the president and various ministers walked in. The idea was to shock them with the extent of the devastation.

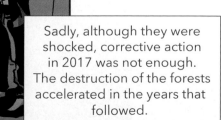

Sadly, although they were shocked, corrective action in 2017 was not enough. The destruction of the forests accelerated in the years that followed.

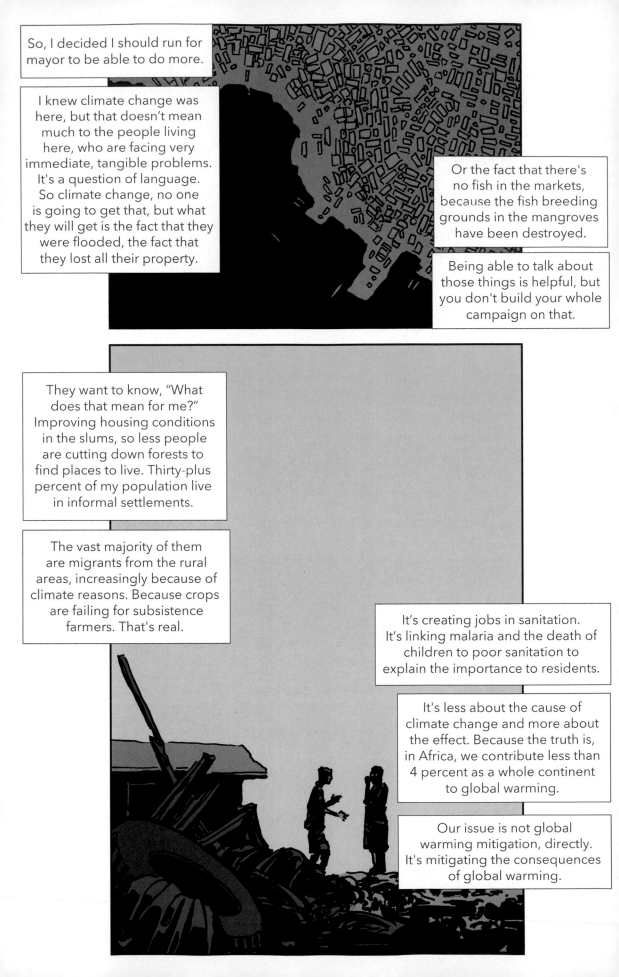

So, I decided I should run for mayor to be able to do more.

I knew climate change was here, but that doesn't mean much to the people living here, who are facing very immediate, tangible problems. It's a question of language. So climate change, no one is going to get that, but what they will get is the fact that they were flooded, the fact that they lost all their property.

Or the fact that there's no fish in the markets, because the fish breeding grounds in the mangroves have been destroyed.

Being able to talk about those things is helpful, but you don't build your whole campaign on that.

They want to know, "What does that mean for me?" Improving housing conditions in the slums, so less people are cutting down forests to find places to live. Thirty-plus percent of my population live in informal settlements.

The vast majority of them are migrants from the rural areas, increasingly because of climate reasons. Because crops are failing for subsistence farmers. That's real.

It's creating jobs in sanitation. It's linking malaria and the death of children to poor sanitation to explain the importance to residents.

It's less about the cause of climate change and more about the effect. Because the truth is, in Africa, we contribute less than 4 percent as a whole continent to global warming.

Our issue is not global warming mitigation, directly. It's mitigating the consequences of global warming.

I suppose what I'm trying to convey is that when you are campaigning to people, you've got to talk about things that impact them. And then it's your job to help them be part of the solution.

Because we mustn't forget, it's the poor who suffer the most from climate change.

We started an initiative called "#FreetowntheTreetown" to provide for paid work planting trees. One million trees.

Our goal is to plant a million trees, including around the water catchment areas to protect those areas. We're putting them on the hillsides to reduce the runoff and allow the water tables to be replenished during the rainy season.

We're planting a million trees, but we're going to need millions more. And we're also going to need the national government to reverse its policy. Its current policy is effectively making it open season for deforestation nationally.

Every year it gets hotter. The city has changed so much. When I was growing up in the mountains, you had to wear a cardigan. My parents never needed air conditioning because it got so cold. It's not that way anymore.

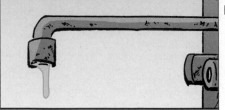

Historically, the city was cool in December, because we have the harmattan blowing from the Sahara desert at night, which makes the temperatures drop. So, in the morning, when the winds were still blowing, everything was cool.

The trees that provided shade are gone. It feels suffocating. It just feels really uncomfortable. The weather patterns are changing.

But now we don't feel the harmattan as much anymore.

Last year, we had one of our lowest rainfalls in history. The water tables for the dam didn't rise to where they should go so that we can have water throughout the year. It's March and there's already almost no water in the taps.

We also joined with other cities and organizations in order to be part of this discourse on extreme heat, this conversation about what we can do. How we should address this silent killer that doesn't get enough attention.

There was an opportunity made by the Adrienne Arsht-Rockefeller Foundation Resilience Center to collaborate with them funding a position of chief heat officer to address extreme heat. And we thought it was a brilliant idea.

So, having Eugenia Kargbo as our chief heat officer means we now have more bandwidth to fight the problems.

Mitigating climate change is a priority of my government. We've passed a sustainability resolution in council just six months ago, and we created for the first time ever a climate change committee of council.

The benefit of having a Chief Heat Officer working with the Resilience Center and having Eugenia connected with counterparts in Athens and Miami is there's an opportunity to share ideas.

One new concept that came out of it that we're trying to adopt is having covers put up in the street markets.

It's still in the design and concept stage. We have 42 markets in the city, only maybe 20 of which are covered places, and the rest are literally street markets, where traders are out in the sun all day.

Sixty percent of our women work in the informal sector, and they are traders. So, the vast majority of the people of Freetown are actually affected by working out in the sun.

It's impossible to know how many people die every year from extreme heat. The statistics here, and health stats, are incredibly poor. No one measures for this stuff. We have a life expectancy of 54. But what are people dying from?

We have 400-plus doctors in our country with a population of 7.5 million people. One of the things we've done is to secure funding to start a postgraduate school for obstetricians and gynecologists because of the high rates of maternal mortality.

Even small adaptations can make big improvements. I will do everything I can to make conditions better for the people I serve.

CHAPTER 9
THE YOUNG ACTIVISTS RISKING FREEDOM FOR THEIR FUTURE

Young people have been experiencing the climate crisis since our childhood. This made us question it instead of accepting it or setting it aside as a "natural disaster." But I do believe that this is an intergenerational problem and that we need everyone to solve it.

Disha Ravi, 24, climate activist, Bengaluru, India

Mayumi Sato, 27, climate justice activist, Cambridge University

I think the effects of climate change are right here on the doorstep for a lot of people, especially in the Global South*. I still think that rich people, especially rich white people, are pretty well protected from the worst of it. But even if you *are* protected, you can still see the increasing effects, at least because of the power of technology and social media. So I think there has been a lot of solidarity building among younger people.

I was born in Japan, but my family originally moved to the U.S. when I was young. We were only supposed to stay a few years, but then my parents split.

*Parts of the world outside North America and Europe, which are referred to as the Global North.

I stayed with my mom and my sister. We moved around all over North America, because my mom's path did not go the way that she thought it was going to go as a single mom with multiple jobs. I ended up finishing high school in Seattle.

I DESERVE A FUTURE

BOYCOTT BANKS!!!!

CAPITALISM IS THE CRISIS

That was right when the Occupy movement was really gaining traction in the city. At the same time, I was taking a summer Arabic language class, and that's the first time I had really learned about the Arab Spring. A few months after that, I remember reading about Trayvon [Martin] and feeling distraught.

I think those movements were the first exposure that I had to social justice.

I went to McGill University in Montreal, but I always wanted to go abroad. I was always envious because a lot of McGill students went overseas to study abroad in their third year of undergrad. I just never had the money to do that.

So I applied to this fellowship program that places recent college graduates in different parts of Asia. I was placed in Chiang Mai with an organization there that works on migrant workers' rights – Shan refugees from Myanmar.

It doesn't get much coverage here, but there are several civil conflicts in Myanmar over natural resources. A lot of the refugees from the Shan state, for instance, go through these secret tunnels and forests to escape.

They find their way in Thailand and then, all of a sudden, they're unemployed. They don't speak the language. They are ostracized. They can't access health services. So I was sent to Chiang Mai first, to help the organization support them.

There was a boy who spoke English, and he was translating between me and the Shan community there. He told me there were lots of natural resources that are incredibly rich in the Shan state, but the military wanted access.

While these civilians are trying to live in the place that they grew up in, the military's kicking them out or killing them. So that's why they have to flee.

My role there was to help the field work staff, to collect data on how many people are beneficiaries of certain programs. Training refugees to plant mushrooms in their gardens or make soap, as examples, so that they can sell it at the market. So that they can rebuild their lives.

Afterward, I joined a local Thai NGO based in Bangkok that focuses on deforestation in the region. One that works with indigenous communities, who basically subsist off natural resources and live with the land, whether that's timber or bamboo. I was specifically attached to the Laos team, so I traveled there.

My goal there became to understand how there are all these different climate policies that are now becoming mandated — especially at the international standard, like the E.U. is doing — telling all these timber-producing countries you need to curb deforestation because it's not sustainable.

That is obviously true, but these policies are also being immediately mandated without understanding how they are going to affect people on the ground. There are all sorts of unintended consequences that happen.

Deforestation has gotten so bad in Laos that the forest cover went from like 70% to 40% in a few decades, and quite a lot of it is attributable to illegal logging. There's also poor government oversight. Bribery is rampant.

Of course, the legal way would be to formalize your timber operations through paperwork and necessary finances. But many small timber operators and laborers are too poor to be able to afford to do that, and these regulations harm them disproportionally. In school, you learn that these climate policies are supposed to be good. But in Laos that's not always true. Sometimes there's way more nuance.

We brought all of that information back to the Laotian government to present a report. We said, we support this policy, but you need to create certain safeguards to make sure that these smaller businesses can transition and not shut down just because they can't conform to these international regulations. And they listened — they simply weren't aware that this was all happening on the ground.

We would inspect their facilities, and we would see laborers who were working there missing a hand from working conditions. This one guy was bleeding right in front of me. Another guy was limping with a crutch. That to me was quite harrowing and disturbing because this is now not even like an SME*, but a large-scale operator. They have the means to protect their workers.

*Small-to-medium enterprise.

They take pride in being able to fulfill all these climate policies and new regulations, but they can be unethical in their approach to employing people. They don't care about injuries. The smaller owners who treat their laborers better are squeezed out. This isn't just a problem in Laos, though — I know it happens all over the world.

I was so frustrated with what I was dealing with in Laos and Thailand, so I was really determined to raise these issues on a broader scale. I loved Laos, but policy changes can take a lot longer to realize. It's hard to create change. So, I decided to try a more international space. I was going to a lot of youth conferences. And then I won a few awards in Germany and the U.S., which gave me the opportunity to work with more policy issues.

Because of my Japanese background, I worked to broach climate activism and gender-related issues with the Ministry of the Environment in Japan.

I'm really privileged because I have this native English accent. When I went into a meeting with these policymakers, I didn't speak to the Minister of Environment in Japanese. I spoke to him in English, as it is my dominant language.

I was invited to the United Nations General Assembly as a youth representative of Japan. All of the world leaders were there. It was such a weird moment to realize you're going from working with people who don't have money to being around the most powerful people in the world.

September, 2019

But it was also disturbing. Every president, every prime minister, is giving speeches patting themselves on the back about what their contribution is to battling climate change. Their contributions included feeling proud of putting solar panels up on the U.N. building, rather than thinking about something far more long-term and ambitious. I remember listening to Boris Johnson talk about how the U.K. is a leader of climate finance and climate policy.

Then when any leader of a lower income country spoke, all of those Global North countries like the U.S., Japan — all of those bigger heads of state — they were not even in the room. They weren't even listening.

So I felt, this is pointless. I could see from a bird's-eye view who was leaving at what points in time. You realize, there's such a disrespect for Global South countries and what they're going through. Even though they're trying to tell these world powers, "This is how we're affected by climate change."

I'm not sure that I've accomplished what I want to yet.

I was really happy about working with people in Laos, being able to understand and report what they're going through. But I left. Now, I feel like it's unfinished business.

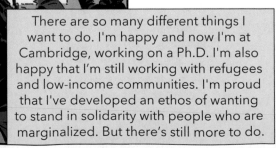

There are so many different things I want to do. I'm happy and now I'm at Cambridge, working on a Ph.D. I'm also happy that I'm still working with refugees and low-income communities. I'm proud that I've developed an ethos of wanting to stand in solidarity with people who are marginalized. But there's still more to do.

For me, my environmental consciousness started with the fact that my grandparents are farmers. They lived three hours from my city in the village, and they didn't have access to a lot of water. And that was because they were highly dependent on groundwater, like most of India.

Even in the city, we had struggles with water. My mother would have to get water from the community wells that we had until they actually placed pipes to bring water inside the house.

There are about 600 million people in the country who are having some sort of water or sanitation crisis, because of how hard it is becoming just to access a very basic need.

I thought this was normal until I was older. I was around 18 when I started asking these questions. I said, "Why is this happening?" There were no real environmental studies in school.

Even when I started understanding about the climate crisis, it was all from the internet, because I didn't have the option to study it in university with my business major. I read so many blogs – 10 Things You Can Do To Be More Sustainable, that sort of thing. But those didn't apply to the problems in my own locality.

I think that's really what made me start working with other citizen groups in my own city that were working on these issues. That's what made me understand that this is a lived reality for us. Climate change is not something that's happening in the future. It's been happening to us for a while now.

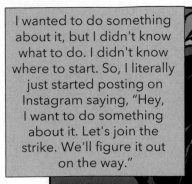

I wanted to do something about it, but I didn't know what to do. I didn't know where to start. So, I literally just started posting on Instagram saying, "Hey, I want to do something about it. Let's join the strike. We'll figure it out on the way."

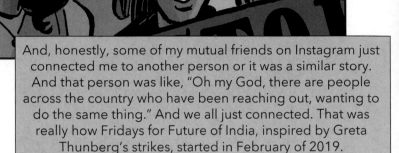

And, honestly, some of my mutual friends on Instagram just connected me to another person or it was a similar story. And that person was like, "Oh my God, there are people across the country who have been reaching out, wanting to do the same thing." And we all just connected. That was really how Fridays for Future of India, inspired by Greta Thunberg's strikes, started in February of 2019.

We said, "Let's do this." And we had our first try. I had it here in Bengaluru. There were strikes in Delhi and Mumbai, too. That was the first time we had a community of people, young people who cared about this. And we worked with other people, older environmentalists who've been trying to do this for years.

So, it started with strikes, but it became a very local issue. We took up issues that were impacting our own cities initially, and then we obviously moved on to national issues.

We had anywhere from 1,500 to 2,000 people show up, and to us that is a huge number. Because unlike the Global North, we don't have any money to organize these strikes. We made our banners from old saris and curtains.

It's also near impossible to get a strike permit given the political situation, which is worsening every single day. If you decide to protest without getting a permit, you could be arrested, beaten, and jailed.

Then in August 2020, the farmers' protests started. The youth climate movement and environmental movements across the country formed a coalition, called Greens Farmers. The "Greens" part was a joke because the local newspapers here call us "greens" derisively, like "tree huggers" in the U.S.

The farmers' protests started because the government passed three new laws that would hurt small farmers in terms of how they can sell their produce, how much money they can make, and to whom they can sell. Small farmers would have to directly compete with big corporations that own big supermarkets.

We recognized how it was important for us to support them, and we recognized that none of us live single-issue lives. This could affect food security and impact climate collapse in the long run.

That is why farmers across the country started protesting. Tens of thousands of famers walked all the way to Delhi, which is the capital of India, because they knew they would at least be heard there. There was a huge outpouring of support nationally and internationally.

Then Greta tweeted about it to her 5 million followers on Feb. 2nd [under the hashtag #Farmersprotest]. That's when I messaged her a link to an online protest toolkit, essentially the information we already had on the motivations of the protests, where the protests were, and how you can support the farmers if you're not from India.

nna ✓

nna - Follow

That was all the online toolkit had. I didn't actually make the kit because a lot of other people contributed to it. There's nothing in it that you'd actually find dangerous. But because Greta ended up tweeting it, it went viral.

The Delhi police and the government were already annoyed that it was getting so much international attention after Rihanna made a previous tweet.

The authorities tried to connect the toolkit to violence that occurred a few days earlier on Jan. 26th.

That is a very important day for us. It is Republic Day in India, when the Constitution came into existence. Some of the farmers had marched on the Red Fort, a very historic landmark in Delhi. On that day, in that place, there was violence between the police and protesters.

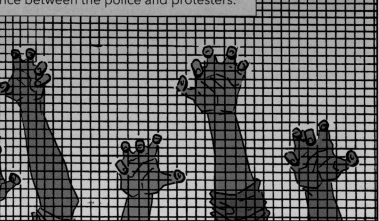

I don't really know exactly what happened since we get polarizing news accounts over here.

I was staying at home as the police announced they were investigating the toolkit as part of a supposed conspiracy. I didn't try to go anywhere, because I knew I was innocent. I didn't even write the tool kit, and there was nothing wrong or illegal in the toolkit. It was just an information dump and I edited two lines. Why would the police arrest me or anyone? It was entirely innocent.

But they just picked me up because they couldn't find anyone else to blame and they had a national uproar. They arrested me. I was terrified because my mom was having, like, a nervous breakdown. She did not know what to do.

NEWS

BREAKING NEWS

FARMER PROTEST 'TOOLKIT' PROBE: 22-YEAR-OLD ARRESTED

...The toolkit stated that its aim was to enable anyone unfamiliar with the ongoing farmers' protests in India to understand the situation...Delhi police, however, say this was part of a conspiracy against the government of India.

Disha Ravi, a 22 year-old college student from Bengaluru, was arrested last night under several charges including sedition, and brought to the capital.

They flew me to Delhi. The whole thing was very scary because I had never been to that part of the country before. I have no family there.

It went on for a month, of which I was in jail for 10 days. After that time, I got bail, but I still had to go to the police station every single day for 10 to 12 hours to be interrogated. For a whole month I didn't see my mother. It was wild.

At least I couldn't be beaten or worse in prison because I was in the news. They couldn't hurt me physically, so they hurt me mentally.

My time in judicial custody was spent in a cell one quarter the size of my room, and there were four people sharing that space.

I didn't know when it was going to end. Because these are serious charges. I had been charged with sedition, which is life in prison if you get convicted.

I thought I would literally die there because I didn't know what was happening. Especially when I was in judicial custody. I couldn't talk to anyone. At least in police custody I could talk to my mother for 10 minutes a day.

I was mad at myself. "This is what I'm arrested for? This is going to be what I'm known for in the news?" Not for doing something that's genuinely worthy. Not for organizing movements to get climate justice. But for sending someone a document?

It's been more than a year and a half, and my case is still ongoing. I am still able to work on my activism, but it's a very conscious choice that I have to make knowing the risks. Knowing that there could be a future arrest on different charges, which would be worse because I have existing charges now.

I actually have no idea on most days what will happen. I want to hope for a better world every single time. I don't want to live in fear that my work is going to get me arrested. But I also don't want to live with the fear that if I don't do anything about the climate crisis that everything is still going to be the same.

I don't believe that it's just going to be me changing the whole entire world. But I do believe that I will have a role to play.

CHAPTER 10
THE ASTRONAUT WHO WANTS TO HELP SAVE EARTH

Climate change happens on such a big, broad scale that you cannot really sense it. The timescale is years. The geographical scales are huge. It's happening across continents.

So, it's really difficult to experience it with your senses. You can reason, you can theorize about climate change. But I think we're basic mammals in what we can perceive.

When I went to space… that's when everything was put into perspective.

**Thomas Pesquet, 44,
European Space Agency**

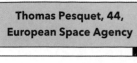

I am an astronaut, and for 400 days*, I could watch the Earth from a 400 kilometer [250 miles] altitude as a crew member on the International Space Station.

*Proxima Mission, flight engineer, Nov. 17, 2016, to June 2, 2017.

Alpha Mission, flight engineer, April 23, 2021, to Nov. 9, 2021.

Named Commander of the ISS on Oct. 4, 2021.

By going into space, taking that step back, putting those phenomena at a scale at which you're able to experience them with your own senses –

– suddenly, you can see the effects of climate change. It makes a big difference, perceiving things with your senses as opposed to just reasoning with your brain. It's a completely different impact.

And that was my experience on my two missions aboard the International Space Station, looking at the Earth from above.

The only thing you can do once you have that realization for yourself is to try to share that perspective. That's why using social media is huge for us. Because we can kind of lend our eyes and our vision to people and say, "Look, this is what we see from the space station. Just see for yourself."

As an astronaut, you are taught how to use a camera at a basic level during training in order to provide Mission Control with pictures of our daily work.

During events like major forest fires, crewmembers on ISS are asked to provide imagery to help relief efforts on the ground. But really, snapping pictures of Earth is a way to use our (limited) free time on ISS.

The scenery is so grand that from day one I was immediately hooked, and decided I had to improve my skills so that I could do justice to the beauty that was unfolding daily in front of my eyes: The oceans, the clouds, the fireworks of colors and shapes that is the Earth from above.

I sort of became the official photographer on board, because of how much time and effort I put into taking pictures, outside and inside ISS, day and night.

I prepared even more for my second mission, putting an endless list of photography targets on an electronic map. The bug caught on with my crewmates, and together we snapped 500,000 pictures in six months!

The fragility of the Earth is also very, very clear in photos.

The effects of human action through water pollution, air pollution, more severe weather phenomena, are very visible from space.

So, you wish everybody could see it for themselves and have that same moment of realization. "Hey, this is real. This is happening!"

This is not something that's very distant in time and space. This is something that's on our doorstep.

Space was always a dream of mine as a kid. I liked planes and space shuttles and I can't really tell you why, because nobody in my family has had any ties to the aerospace world. I played astronaut with my older brother.

One of my first childhood memories is spending hours in a makeshift cardboard space shuttle, equipped with a wicker steering wheel, dials, and gauges drawn in pencil on a cardboard flap that was my instrument panel, and some pillows to sit comfortably during intergalactic travel. All courtesy of my dad.

I studied math and physics, and became an aerospace engineer because that was something that I could grasp. Becoming an astronaut? That was something I had no real idea that you could do.

Being a private pilot, I decided to take the next step and become a professional pilot. And then the European astronaut selection happened. A friend of mine told me I should apply, though I initially thought, "No, it's probably way too difficult." But I did my best and I got in.

Making it to space is a combination of so much work and sacrifice, and there's so much that can happen to prevent you from going — politically, technically, and medically. You have to stay in good health up until the very last moment.

You invest everything in that goal, but you're never quite sure that it's going to happen. Only as you get closer to launch does it become more and more real.

As the launch approaches, you have to say goodbye to your family. It's a very intense moment because even though the risks are mastered most of the time, you make sure that you told them everything you wanted to tell them.

The elevator to the top of the rocket felt like it lasted forever. It's not very fast, and a Soyuz rocket is 53 meters [apx. 174 feet]. I remember that distinct feeling, that it's much higher than I thought it was.

It's very claustrophobic inside the capsule because it's a very small, cramped space and it's full of stuff. You're strapped in shoulder-to-shoulder with the other crew members. Then they close the hatch on you. That big metallic sound. Which I think if you're claustrophobic, is the time when you decide you're not going.

When the rocket lifts off, it's like a kick in the butt.

As soon as you clear the pad and everything is nominal* though, you get the feeling that it's going to be okay. It's constant gradual acceleration. So, you're squashed in your seat. You're monitoring all the instruments. It's vibrating, but the sound is not too bad. You can hear mission control.

*All systems are within acceptable parameters for launch, and the weather is favorable.

The acceleration is from 0 to 100 kilometers [apx. 62.1 miles], when you add 100 kilometers per hour every two seconds. It's faster than a Formula One car, but over the course of almost nine minutes of acceleration!

You feel like you're on a cloud as soon as you reach orbit and the engines stop pushing. You start floating in weightlessness, a huge change from the crushing feeling of the launch.

And that's going to be the feeling for 200 days, until you come back to Earth.

I think that the first visual that I really remember and that kind of shocks me in certain ways is how thin the atmosphere is.

Because if you look straight down at the Earth, you don't see it. But if you look sideways, over the horizon, you see a bubble, and that's really a thin, thin layer of air. That's just how small the atmosphere is.

It's only a few dozen kilometers. That's all that protects us from the void of space. All the life that we ever knew is maintained within that layer that's surrounding the Earth. It looks like a soap bubble. That's how fragile it looks.

Snapping pictures was not one of the main parts of my job description on the ISS.

There were science experiments to do, station systems to maintain, and the occasional spacewalk.

And of course, building international friendship. In space, we have to cooperate because no nation in the world, nobody can do it alone. Because that's the scale of these projects. We are talking about going to the moon; we're talking about big space stations in low Earth orbit; we're talking about going to Mars one day. You have to cooperate; there's just no other way.

We have big problems to overcome together. I remember seeing California engulfed by smoke. We could, in some instances, see the actual flames from the orbit. These fires are getting bigger. I had never seen anything like that on my first mission.

I published a photo on social media where you can see the smoke advancing like a shadow or cloud over California, hundreds of miles across.

One of my crewmates, Megan McArthur, is originally from California, and her family was close by to a wildfire. I remember she was emailing back and forth with her dad, who was saying, "Yeah, if the fires are coming really close to the lake, we'll go on the boat and we'll be fine."

She was trying to tell them, "Look, you're not going to be fine judging from what we see from up here." I think eventually the fires were diverted or didn't go all the way out to the home, but it was scary.

We could also see hurricanes forming in the Gulf of Mexico. We could see two or three following each other one after another and heading toward land.

You could look straight down the eye. I took a couple of pictures in which you could see the walls, which I think were 10 to 15 kilometers [apx. 6.2 to 9.3 miles] high. We know hurricanes are getting more destructive when they make landfall because of climate change.

Day after day, we could see them brewing and then heading toward land. You have this feeling of helplessness, but there's nothing you can do. Those were strange moments for us.

You can see the cuts in the Amazon very, very clearly from the space station. Without the trees and their roots, erosion and sedimentation pollute the rivers.

You can also see air pollution over big cities and water pollution in rivers and oceans. The evidence is there in the pictures. But we also have fleets of satellites, you know, providing data on every aspect – water temperature, greenhouse gases, concentration in the atmosphere.

The conclusion on climate change is obvious.

With that big of an experience also comes big responsibility, right?

I didn't feel comfortable coming back home, and you know, start resuming life as usual.

If I was lucky enough to see all this, if I was lucky enough to experience all this, I had to share that experience. Because not everybody can get that perspective that I was so fortunate to get.

So, I started talking about the need to protect the Earth, to kids and to the general public. I think today for the most part, in Europe at least, people are very receptive to those messages.

We know there's a problem. We understand the magnitude and the causes, and what's at stake. The next question is, how do we solve it?

I also have access to decision makers sometimes. And that's the same kind of message that I've tried to get across.

I met the president of France [François Hollande] after he organized the COP21* in Paris and shortly before my first flight. He gave me a copy of the [Paris] agreement to take to space with me.

*Landmark 2015 Paris Climate Conference.

I knew about the conference, of course, but chatting with my fellow countryman had me realize the tireless dedication, patience, and meticulousness needed to get all the countries in the world to negotiate. There were a million times when the organizers could have given up, but they kept pushing.

Today when I talk to leaders, including his successor [Emmanuel Macron], I still use this as an example of difficult, sometimes unpopular actions that are needed from those in power to improve the situation.

Climate change knows no borders, right? So, there's no point in having one country take some measures if the next neighboring country is doing the exact opposite. It's just not going to work.

I guess we have that experience of working together from the ISS. It's certainly more complicated, more difficult on a larger scale.

But we've been working on creating those bonds, creating that friendship. One that's going to last a long time and resist the crises that are going to come our way.

I'm trying not to be naive because I don't believe in that, you know, that magic wand of technology that's going to solve all the problems.

But on the other hand, I remember I had the exact same feeling when I saw the International Space Station for the first time. It's the most complex object ever made, the size of a football field, assembled in the harshest environment that exists, by Japanese, European, American, and Russian engineers working on a common cause.

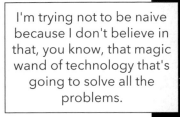

So, when you see this, it should make you reasonably optimistic. If we can do this, then we have the potential to solve the problems of climate change.

We have this ability as a species …if we react now in a massive and immediate way.

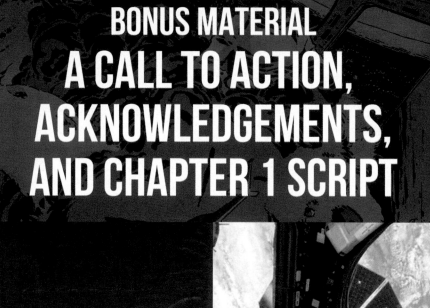

BONUS MATERIAL
A CALL TO ACTION, ACKNOWLEDGEMENTS, AND CHAPTER 1 SCRIPT

A CALL TO ACTION

by **TERRY TAMMINEN, KRISTINA HADDAD, JENNA CITTADINO,** *and* **ETHAN SACKS**

It is not hyperbole to view climate change as the single greatest existential threat in human history. The looming crisis seems so vast that it is natural to feel powerless under its weight.

To mitigate this climate crisis requires societal change of unprecedented scope, including the urgent need for major shifts away from fossil fuels and for leadership from political figures who are dedicated to environmental reform. We can vote, but few of us are in a position to affect policy on such a vast scale ourselves.

We, however, are not powerless. Each and every reader holding this volume can make a difference.

The ten profiles you just read have a common theme: That one person can make a tangible contribution toward improving the present and the future. It doesn't have to be as extreme as battling wildfires or governing a heat-stricken city. If enough people adopt a few more green-conscious habits, the cumulative effect would go a long way toward mitigating the impact of climate change in the years to come.

Here are some ways you can help:

 Wash your clothes in cold. By washing with cold water, you can save on average 90% of the energy you use for every load of laundry, according to the U.S. government's ENERGY Star program.

 Replace your grass with native drought-tolerant plants. This can support animal habitats, promote biodiversity, and save water. Add some more joy to your home by checking out the Audubon Society's Native Plant Database to learn about the best native plants for birds in your area.

 Switch to green power. As a residential customer, you can choose to purchase renewable energy for your household. If your electricity company doesn't offer the option directly, you can purchase renewable energy through Renewable Energy Certificates (RECs). Green-e is an organization that certifies REC providers and offers a database and links to suppliers on green-e.org.

 Fly nonstop when possible and choose economy class. Direct flights use less carbon emissions than connecting flights. When factoring in the additional airplane emissions produced from landing and taking off, as well as the extra distance, nonstop is a better way to go whenever possible. Flying economy is also better for the environment, as the flight's carbon emissions are shared among more passengers.

Go meatless one day a week. Skipping red meat is not just good for your health. It is also good for the environment. Cows release methane, a potent greenhouse gas, and oxygen-producing forests are destroyed in the conversion to grazing lands for cattle raising. Livestock also bring a whole host of other resource, chemical, pollution, disease, and cruelty issues. Skipping meat just one day a week can make a positive environmental impact.

Avoid plastic cutlery and straws, and bring your own coffee cups. According to the EPA, only 8.7% of plastics were recycled, while 27 million tons of the non-biodegradable material ended up in landfills. Instead of adding to the problem, consider using reusable cutlery kits that you can purchase online. Avoid plastic straws and stirrers, which often end up in the ocean, endangering wildlife. Finally, most disposable coffee cups are lined with plastic and aren't biodegradable, so it's better to opt for a reusable cup instead.

Volunteer for an environmental group and advocate for the Earth in your community. Connect with like-minded people, all while helping the environment. You can also extend your positive influence on global warming well beyond your home by actively encouraging others to take action.

Some examples of places to start:

• **Carbon-Free Campus** (carbonfreecampus.org) is a program that helps schools reduce their carbon emissions and adopt a sustainable lifestyle at home.

• **Grades of Green** (gradesofgreen.org) offers "environmental leadership training" and project-based learning about various environmental lessons for grades K-12.

• **ClimatePartner Online Academy** (climatepartner.com) helps businesses create a climate action strategy.

• **Earthday.org** created a Teach-In Toolkit to help you advocate for climate action in your community.

Vote! Let your voice be heard and vote for representatives who prioritize the battle against climate change. Support candidates who will take action to phase out fossil fuels and protect our planet.

Terry Tamminen is the CEO of AltaSea at the Port of Los Angeles, a nonprofit dedicated to fighting climate change and protecting our oceans. Previously, he served as Secretary of the California Environmental Protection Agency, as well as CEO of the Leonardo DiCaprio Foundation. His books include "Cracking the Carbon Code: The Keys to Sustainable Profits in the New Economy" and "Lives Per Gallon: The True Cost of Our Oil Addiction."

Kristina Haddad is the Executive Director of 7th Generation Advisors, a nonprofit based on the ancient First Nations philosophy that the decisions we make today should result in a sustainable world seven generations into the future. She has over two decades of experience working in the environmental nonprofit sector, including serving on several boards.

Jenna Cittadino is the Programs Director of 7th Generation Advisors and has compiled over one hundred practical actions that everyone can take to solve climate change and protect future generations (those listed here are just a few).

ACKNOWLEDGEMENTS

This book may have Dalibor, Lee, and my names on the cover, but it took the efforts of dozens of people to help make it happen.

In appropriate terms for a comic book, this volume of real-life accounts of people on the front lines of the battle against climate change around the world has an origin story.

It began two and a half years ago in New York City. When my city shut down in March 2020 at the beginning of the COVID pandemic, AWA Studios CCO and fellow New Yorker **Axel Alonso** reached out to me to use the comic medium to spotlight a different kind of hero.

As someone who owes his start in comics to Axel, he had me at hello. As a journalist turned comic book writer, I immediately grasped on to his vision. Instead of capes and cowls, we opted to focus on the do-gooders donning surgical PPE to risk their lives to save others in those early, most dangerous days of the pandemic.

Axel paired me up with artist **Dalibor Talajic**, one of the heavyweight talents at his craft.

The result, *Covid Chronicles*, ran on the NBC News website, winning a New York Press Club Award in the process. The trade paperback, graced with the glorious

PHOTO BY NINA LIN

by
ETHAN SACKS

colors of **Lee Loughridge**, earned further acclaim.

That success paved the way for a spiritual sequel.

And I knew exactly the topic I wanted to tackle this time around.

Climate Crisis Chronicles would focus on the devastating effects of the greatest threat in human history on a global scale—but show it through the eyes of individuals who are on the front lines of that crisis. The goal: To show these forces that can seem abstract or too gargantuan to comprehend on a personal and intimate scale.

The resulting series has reunited me with Dalibor and Lee. Their painstaking work to match the accuracy of dozens of reference photos and filling in the blanks

with additional research was essential. This series would not have succeeded as well in any other hands.

Once again, I am indebted to the ace editorial team at AWA Studios for their guidance and dedication to an ambitious project. As she did with *Covid Chronicles*, editor **Dulce Montoya** provided a steadying hand and a careful eye on making sure this series was the best it could be.

Editors **Michael Coast** and **Thea Cheuk** were also major pillars who propped up *Climate Crisis Chronicles* from the first planning emails to the finished volume you hold in your hands. **Bosung Kim**, another veteran of the first series, returned to grace this project with her exceptional lettering. Letterers are the unsung heroes of comics, and Bosung's praises must be sung from the rooftops.

Marketing guru **Jackie Liu** helped get the word out, an all-important mission on a project of this scale. **Chris Burns** supplied yeoman work on production, and **Chris Ferguson** contributed the stellar design. **Yeonjung Kim** converted the series from digital to trade, a mammoth task.

I am humbled by the support of NBC News Digital, under the leadership of

the great **Catherine Kim**, who championed both *Climate Crisis Chronicles* and its predecessor from the earliest of stages. Having had the honor of spending several years working in that newsroom, I hold NBC News in the highest of regards. The honor of being hosted on one of the largest, and best, news sites in the world was invaluable to our message of sharing this unique look at the devastating impact of climate change far and wide.

I owe the biggest debt of gratitude to **Meredith Bennett-Smith**, the editor of the esteemed NBC News Think section. Meredith's tireless efforts and leadership are the primary reasons that the online version of this series was published on time despite the tightest of deadlines. That I accidentally omitted her from the acknowledgements on *Covid Chronicles* bothers me to this day. So, let me rectify that error by now thanking her here for her contributions to that series as well.

Her colleagues, **Elise Wrabetz**, **Nigel Chiwaya**, **JoElla Carman**, and **Ned Kilkelly**, did the heavy lifting of getting these webpages up and running on extremely tight deadlines, and of copy editing each and every caption. If I left anyone off of the list this time, I apologize profusely.

Having **Al Roker**, the me-

teorologist whose weather reports for the Today Show were a staple in my household for almost four decades, write the foreword is a humbling honor. That he immediately got the am-

> **Climate Crisis Chronicles would focus on the devastating effects of the greatest threat in human history on a global scale—but show it through the eyes of individuals who are on the front lines of that crisis.**

bitions of *Climate Crisis Chronicles* is all the proof I need that we are on the right track. I am grateful to **Briana Watson** of NBC News for quarterbacking the efforts.

After getting the green light, the scramble to find profile subjects that could properly convey both the enormity and universality of climate change began. This book is the result of months of reporting and interviews. It is also the result of trust by the participants, and a shared belief in the importance of the cause of sharing their experiences.

For the first chapter, I wanted to focus on a California firefighter who had experience battling wildfires long enough to see the effect cli-

mate change is having over time. I am indebted to **Jon Heggie** of Cal Fire for seeing the potential of this project and enlisting the perfect profile subject. I am indebted to **Mark Brunton** for sharing his vast experience, and as well as his very personal, harrowing memories.

Johanna Reina of the United Nations High Commissioner for Refugees office not only helped me track down the perfect subject for a chapter on how climate change is already impacting life in Central America, she served tirelessly as a translator when I spoke with **Lucita Hernandez**. **Marcela Martinez**, **Danielle Alvarez**, and **Marco Goncalves Dias** provided statistics and reports, and further assistance from the ground. As for Lucita herself, her tireless dedication to her community in the face of grave danger is awe-inspiring.

Illustrating the melting of arctic ice in a way that would captivate readers would be a challenge in this format. So, I opted to show the effects on animals directly impacted by the arctic crisis. **Alysa McCall** of The Polar Bears International proved the perfect guide to conditions on the ground in Churchill, Manitoba. One of the many hats (toques) she wears is as the organization's director of conservation outreach, and thus proved a deft teacher to this eager student.

(Continued on Page 98)

I found the subject of Chapter 4, **Taimi Amutse**, with the help of American Red Cross International communications lead **Susan Malandrino**. As for Taimi herself, her patience at trekking to the regional office for better reception for our interviews was especially appreciated. Her joy from the important work she does for others is impressive and infectious.

Impressed by his stunning photos, I reached out to **Ian Teh**. His keen eye made him the perfect guide to put the ravages of the Chinese coal industry into focus. I strongly recommend visiting ianteh.com to see for yourself.

Having read about the plight of koala bears during the horrific brushfires across Australia in 2019-2020, I combed articles and video reports to find a potential expert who could speak to the scale of the calamity. I am grateful to **Claire Agnew**, then communications manager for the New South Wales-based Friends of the Koala, for introducing me to **Ros Irwin**. I hope the sixth chapter hopefully does justice to her passion and commitment to these beloved, but endangered, animals.

My good friend, **Rebecca Scheurer**, then the director of humanitarian initiatives at the Adrienne Arsht-Rockefeller Foundation Resilience Center, selflessly talked through several potential stories centered around extreme heat. Chapters 7 and 8 come directly out of those conversations. I am in awe of her dedication and institutional knowledge, and extremely proud of the good work she continues to do. I am proud of my friend.

The most ambitious chapter in this book may be the one focusing on the important mission of the crew of the Ocean Viking, as they rescue migrants making a perilous attempt to cross the Mediterranean in boats. The joint operation undertaken by SOS Mediterranee, and the International Federation of Red Cross and Red Crescent Societies, has complexities that required multiple perspectives. That, in turn, took assistance coordinating from a raft of helpers, including **Claire Junet** of SOS Mediterranee, and **Zeke Simperingham**, **Bob Ghosn**, and **Anna Tuson** at the IFRC.

PHOTO BY KAMILA JANCZYK

COURTESY OF DISHA RAVI

Top: Yvonne Aki-Sawyerr, the mayor of Freetown, observes a poor neighborhood in her city. Above: Activist Disha Ravi at a climate protest.

In the coming years we will see an increasing number of migrants displaced by the ravages of climate change, whether from fires, floods, or droughts. The dedication of people like **Maria Munoz-Bertrand**, **Francesco Fornari**, and **Olivier** gives me some hope.

In an era in which many political figures in the Global North struggle to pass watered-down green policies--or even deny climate change all together--Freetown mayor **Yvonne Aki-Sawyerr** is a role model of true leadership. That she gave so much of her time to our project despite her myriad of responsibilities is a gift we do not take for granted. **Mauricio Rodas** and **Fatmata Kanyako** facilitated the interview.

The sheer scale of the crisis is paralyzing for many. But not to the young Millennial and Gen Z activists who are dedicating their lives to affecting positive change. **Disha Ravi** risked much to speak with me in the aftermath of her arrest. Spreading the message of environmental activism, however, is important enough for her to take that chance. **Mayumi Sato** has done important work from the jungles of Laos to the hallways of the United Nations. They are among numerous inspirations to my daughter's generation.

For the final chapter, I opted for an aerial view of the

Astronaut Thomas Pesquet in his perch on the International Space Station. Pesquet took photographic evidence of the ravages of wildfires, superstorms, and deforestation.

COURTESY OF ESA/NSA

problems of climate change to put it all into perspective. Who better than astronaut **Thomas Pesquet**, who took photographic evidence of the ravages of wildfires, superstorms, and deforestation from his perch on the International Space Station? With the help of **Adelaide Thomas** of the European Space Agency, I was able to track him down on Earth and enlist him into our mission.

Behind the scenes, I am grateful for the guidance of my friend, **Terry Tamminen**, who was my supervisor and mentor during my volunteer stint at the Leonardo DiCaprio Foundation. Now the president/CEO of the AltaSea project at the Port of Los Angeles, Terry gave feedback that helped shape the direction of the book. He and his staffers at 7th Generation Advisors, **Kristina Haddad** and **Jenna Cittadino**, helped me craft a call to action to end the volume. The hope is that these ten stories will inspire you, the reader, to join the battle, armed with practical tips on how to do so.

Among Terry's many gifts to this book was an introduction to **Dr. Michael Mann**, one of the preeminent experts in the field of climate science. Despite an inhumanly packed schedule, he made time to offer suggestions and his support on social media. As cliché as it sounds, Michael truly is a gentleman and a scholar.

Last but not least, I thank you the reader for taking the time to take a look. Your support helped Axel's initial vision of illustrated journalism go from a cocktail napkin idea to the printed page.
— Ethan Sacks,
New York City,
October 2022

CLIMATE CRISIS CHRONICLES
CHAPTER 1

NOTE: There are a lot of reference photos included, but the artist should have some artistic license to not have to replicate all of them exactly. It's more for visual understanding.

Panel 1. A tight shot of Cal Fire battalion chief Mark Brunton in a helicopter, seated by the side opposite the pilot, looking out of the window, down at something that's off panel. Mark is wearing a helmet and visor. We'll see a much clearer shot of his face in a few panels. In the meantime, let's zoom in close enough that we don't have to worry about seeing any identifying number for a specific copter. Let's make sure we have different color captions for the narration vs. locators or descriptors.

> CAPTION:
> Mark Brunton, 52, Battalion Chief, Cal Fire

> CAPTION: (Narration)
> I've been a firefighter for 36 years. I've been on the Cal Fire Incident Management Team for about 20 of them.

> CAPTION: (Narration)
> Wildfires have been a part of a job since I started.

> CAPTION: (Narration)
> But where it really took off was in the last five years.

 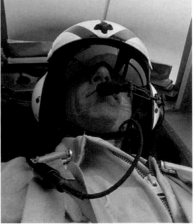

Panel 2. Flip the perspective to look down over the helicopter at an aerial view of the tree-lined ridge below, where a wall of fire is spreading. The swathe of destruction is terrifying. Let's keep the dialogue short to really play off the scale of the image.

        CAPTION: (Narration)
That's when we started seeing fires that were significantly bigger.

        CAPTION:
The Dixie Fire, August, 2021.

Panel 3. A generic shot of a Cal Fire firefighter or firefighters silhouetted by a wall of flames.

        CAPTION: (Narration)
We've been in a historic drought for the past few years in California.

        CAPTION: (Narration)
We're finding that the vegetation is very dry. Conditions that are fuel for bigger wildfires.

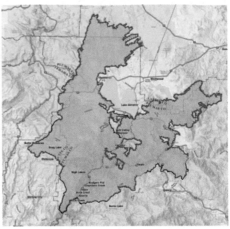

Panel 4. Now we're getting our first good look at Mark as he stands in front of a map during a briefing. Let's be clear not to copy the detail on the map behind him exactly as that's from a different fire in that reference photo.
Just in case the artist wants to be very authentic with the Dixie Fire, this is what it looked like in August from a shape perspective.

CAPTION: (Narration)
I am the operation section chiefs on one of three incident teams at Cal Fire.

CAPTION: (Narration)
My team started working the Dixie Fire about three weeks after it started, rotating in for the first team.

CAPTION: (Narration)
As the wildfire season gets longer, Cal Fire has been trying to everything they can to give firefighters time to recuperate.

CAPTION: (Narration)
Last year there was a stretch I worked 92 days in a row myself.

Panel 5. Mark is giving a pep talk, something like a Braveheart speech, to a small group of fire fighters.

CAPTION: (Narration)
There are many things over my career that have motivated me to do what I do, and do what others I work with do.

CAPTION: (Narration)
There are a lot of rabid Notre Dame football fans on my team, so I like to quote Lou Holtz at the operational briefing.

CAPTION: (Narration)
"It's not the load that breaks you down, it's the way you carry it."

Panel 6. A sea of tents is visible, but the entire area of the hazy from smoke.

> CAPTION: (Narration)
> I'm in charge of about 3,000 people for that three week period.

> CAPTION: (Narration)
> Our logistics folks do a great job, setting up a mini-city. Meals. Laundry. Sleeping facilities. Trailers for offices.

> CAPTION: (Narration)
> The closest the fire actually got to the camp is about 50 miles or so, but everything is smoked in. We didn't see the sun for about three weeks.

Panel 7. A pre-dawn meeting. This time seen as a much wider shot that shows more. This time, a wider shot so we see a lot firefighters listening for a briefing.

> CAPTION: (Narration)
> I have two different deputy operation supervisors who oversee a huge sector of the fire, and underneath them are branches and the divisions.

> CAPTION: (Narration)
> We usually start with meetings early in the morning. You get a download from whoever is doing night operations, about what happened overnight. There's a formal operations briefing for all the resources fighting fire that day. Then it's time to go out and start doing the job for the day.

Panel 8. Aerial view scale of a ridge, with the wildfire spreading across it. A shadow of a helicopter falls on the ground.

> CAPTION: (Narrator)
> After the meetings, there's a small window of time for a recon flight.

> CAPTION: (Narrator)
> It gives me a chance to see the sheer power of the fire, how quickly and thoroughly it consumes trees, brush and structures on such a large scale. A recon flight can take well over an hour to fly only a portion of the fire.

> CAPTION: (Narration)
> I can feel the heat radiate though I am hundreds of feet above the flames.

Panel 9. A shot of the fire ravaging its way through trees.

> CAPTION: (Narration)
> By the time my team came into the Dixie Fire, it has been burning for weeks.

> CAPTION: (Narration)
> A lot of the fire was on steep terrain, heavy timber, with unprecedented runs of thousands or tens of thousands of acres burned in a 24 hour period.

> CAPTION: (Narration)
> None of us had ever seen a fire burn with that intensity.

Panel 10. Firefighters are clearing dry vegetation near a roadway. A dozer pushes more vegetation out of the way in the background.

> CAPTION: (Narration)
> How do you begin to fight a fire that big?

> CAPTION:
> We remind our fire leadership in daily briefings that this is a marathon, not a sprint.

> CAPTION:
> You start by putting in control lines at rivers, ridges or roads in the path of the wildfire. We use dozers and troops put in these huge swathes of fire breaks.

Panel 11. A helicopter flies overhead to drop red fire retardant over a trees.

> CAPTION: (Narration)
> We also use aircraft to drop retardant.

> CAPTION: (Narration)
> It's not called "extinguishant" for a reason. It's a retardant. It slows down the advance of the fire.

Panel 12. Firefighters are lighting more controlled, smaller fires to burn off vegetation.

> CAPTION: (Narration)
> From those lines, we do a backburn type operation.

> CAPTION: (Narration)
> So that's where we use that control line to light a controlled fire.

Panel 13. A wider shot of the backburn fire being set by several firefighters.

       CAPTION: (Narration)
The backburn fire consumes the fuel between the fireline and the wildfire.

       CAPTION: (Narration)
That way when the wildfire burns up to that area it runs out of fuel and goes out or it lowers in intensity.

Panel 14. The fire fighters are hosing down dying flames. The wildfire, here at least, is being extinguished.

       CAPTION: (Narration)
Then we can get in there and use hose-lines to extinguish the flames.

       CAPTION: (Narration)
It takes a lot of time, especially if you're in timber. It takes days. Your line has to be quite large. You need a lot of resources to make it work.

Panel 15. Cut to a newscast showing the town of Greenville, California, having been. We can avoid the branding of a specific news outlet, but it would be good to keep the lettering of the chyron (lower third) in the image.

      CAPTION: (Narration)
The Dixie Fire was the second largest fire in California history acreage wise, pushing almost a million acres.

      CAPTION: (Narration)
Fortunately, the fire burned across a pretty rural area. But it wiped out an entire community with the exception of one building. It wasn't a large town, maybe a couple of thousand people, but the fire just leveled it.

AIO FILMZ

THE NEWS WITH SHEPARD SMITH

DIXIE FIRE DESTROYS HISTORIC CALIFORNIA TOWN OF GREENVILLE

CNBC

Panel 16. Cut to a picture of Mark's uncle's house in happier times. Before the Napa Valley fire.

       CAPTION: (Narration)
I know the devastation of wildfires all too well.

       CAPTION: (Narration)
Last year, in Napa, the fire actually burned down my uncle's home.

       CAPTION: (Narration)
That was surreal. When you kind of have a connection to it.

Panel 17. Cut to an after shot: The house is gone, burned completely to ash and debris.

       CAPTION: (Narration)
It's a terrible thing to see when there are communities wiped out, but when it becomes a personal thing, that brings it home.

       CAPTION: (Narration)
Oh man, I've been in that home. It's pretty devastating.

Panel 18. A picture of Mark's son and wife.

> CAPTION: (Narration)
> My son is in the Navy, and while he protects our country, I am protecting our home state from wildfires.

> CAPTION: (Narration)
> My priority is to keep California safe and to safely return to my family.

Panel 19. A tight shot of Mark behind the wheel of his Cal Fire truck. It's very smokey around hm.

> CAPTION: (Narration)
> That isn't guaranteed. I've had a few close encounters.

> CAPTION: (Narration)
> In the 2017 Thomas Fire in Southern California, I got cut off by the fire when it just took off. I had to try to make it to one of the preset safety islands.

> CAPTON: (Narration)
> The fire was burning across the road, but I couldn't see. I had to gun it.

Panel 20. A truck is driving through a gauntlet of flames on a smoky road. Visibility is almost zero.

> CAPTION: (Narration)
> I couldn't remember what the road was like. I just hoped it doesn't take a turn, or I'd fly off a cliff.

> CAPTION: (Narration)
> But I got through it, got to the safety island and basically waited it out for two hours while the fire burned around me. That was close.

Panel 21. A profile shot of Mark surveying a scene. Firefighters in the background are seen tending to the remnant of a fire. It's been mostly put out.

> CAPTION: (Narration)
> Fires now are so much more devasting than they used to be.

> CAPTON: (Narration)
> It's a grind. The fire season is longer as it gets hotter and drier. You're going from fire to fire. I'll have a day off then it's off to the next one.

> CAPTION: (Narration)
> It's like Groundhog Day.

> CAPTION: (Narration)
> You have to take the wins where you get them.